Certain Chance

Seguro Azar

Pedro Salinas

CERTAIN CHANCE

Poems by
Pedro Salinas

Versions & Introduction
David Lee Garrison

Prologue   Pedro Salinas
Reminiscence   Willis Barnstone
Art   David Leach

Lewisburg
Bucknell University Press
London : Associated University Presses

© 2000 Spanish text by Heirs of Pedro Salinas
© 2000 English translation by Associated University Presses, Inc.

All rights reserved. Authorization to photocopy items for internal or personal use, or the internal or personal use of specific clients, is granted by the copyright owner, provided that a base fee of $10.00, plus eight cents per page, per copy is paid directly to the Copyright Clearance Center, 222 Rosewood Drive, Danvers, Massachusetts 01923. [0-8387-5457-0/00 $10.00 + 8¢ pp, pc.]

Associated University Presses
440 Forsgate Drive
Cranbury, NJ 08512

Associated University Presses
16 Barter Street
London WC1A 2AH, England

Associated University Presses
P.O. Box 338, Port Credit
Mississauga, Ontario
Canada L5G 4L8

The paper used in this publication meets the requirements of the American National Standard for Permanence of Paper for Printed Library Materials Z39.48-1984.

Library of Congress Cataloging-in-Publication Data

Salinas, Pedro, 1891–1951.
 [Seguro azar. English and Spanish]
 Certain chance : poems of Pedro Salinas / Pedro Salinas ; versions and introduction by David Lee Garrison ; prologue by the poet ; reminiscence by Willis Barnstone ; art by David Leach.
   p. cm.
 Includes bibliographical references.
 ISBN 0-8387-5457-0 (alk. paper)
 1. Salinas, Pedro, 1891–1951. I. Garrison, David Lee. II. Title.
PQ6635.A32 S413   2000
862'.62—dc21
                                                         99-058602

PRINTED IN THE UNITED STATES OF AMERICA

for my friend
Willis Barnstone
friend of Pedro Salinas

Contents

Acknowledgments	11
Prologue by the Poet	13
Prólogo del poeta	19
A Life Because of Pedro Salinas by Willis Barnstone	25
Translator's Introduction	31

Seguro azar

Certain Chance

1. *Cuartilla* Page	40
2. *Figuraciones* Imaginings	42
3. *Otra tú* Another You	44
4. *Vocación* Vocation	46
5. *Pasajero apresurado* Hurried Traveler	50
6. *El zumo* Juice	52
7. *Sin voz, desnuda* Without Voice, Naked	54
8. *Fecha cualquiera* Could Be Any Day	56
9. *El mal invitado* The Greedy Guest	58

10. *Navacerrada, abril* Navacerrada, April	60
11. *Orilla* Shore	62
12. *Tránsito* Transition	64
13. *Los equívocos* Illusions	66
14. *Quietud* Peacefulness	70
15. *Far West* Far West	74
16. *Dominio* Dominion	78
17. *Los mares* Oceans	80
18. *Don de la materia* The Gift of Matter	82
19. *Valle* Valley	88
20. *La difícil* Difficult Woman	90
21. *Placer, a las once* Pleasure, at Eleven O'Clock	92
22. *Números* Numbers	94
23. *"Route Nationale"* "Route Nationale"	96
24. *La distraída* Distracted Woman	98
25. *Madrid. Calle de . . .* Madrid. Any Street	100
26. *Cinematógrafo* Movie Theater	102

27. *35 bujías* 35 Candle Power	108
28. *Soledades de la obra* Solitudes of Creation	110
29. *Más* More	112
30. *Inminencia* Imminence	114
31. *Clave de febrero* The Key to February	116
32. *Acuarela* Watercolor	118
33. *Amada exacta* Lover Beside Me	120
34. *La concha* Conch	122
35. *Sur, con viento* South, with Wind	124
36. *Mirar lo invisible* Looking at the Invisible	126
37. *Nivel preferido* Favorite Altitude	130
38. *Lo olvidado* Forgotten	134
39. *Sí reciente* Recent Yes	136
40. *Aviso* Warning	138
41. *Busca, encuentro* Seeking, Finding	140
42. *Marco* Frame	142
43. *El árbol menos* The Missing Tree	144

44. *Atalanta* Atalanta	146
45. *Pasillo de la prisa* Path of Haste	150
46. *Los despedidos* Goodbyes	152
47. *Fe mía* My Faith	154
48. *Amiga* Friend	156
49. *Playa* Beach	158
50. *Triunfo suyo* His Triumph	162
Bibliography	164
Books of Poems by Pedro Salinas	167

Acknowledgments

Previous Publication

Some of these translations were first published in the following magazines: *Asylum*, *Black River Review*, *Blue Unicorn*, *Colorado Review*, *International Poetry Review*, *Nexus*, *Poetry East*, and *Whole Notes*.

Spanish Texts

The text for the Spanish poems has been taken from the edition by the poet's daughter, Soledad Salinas de Marichal, *Poesías completas* (Barcelona: Barral, 1971). The text for the "Prólogo del poeta" comes from her edition of the poet's *Ensayos completos*, III (Madrid: Taurus, 1983), where it appears under the title, "Prólogo a una traducción de sus poemas" (427–30). It was composed by Salinas for Eleanor L. Turnbull's translation of a selection of his early work, *Lost Angels and Other Poems* (Baltimore: The Johns Hopkins University Press, 1938), and it appeared in that volume in her translation but not in Spanish. In the Spanish text printed here with my own translation, I have taken the liberty of deleting or altering a few sentences that pertain to the Turnbull book.

Appreciation

I would like to express my gratitude to the Salinas family and the Mercedes Casanovas Literary Agency for permission to translate *Seguro azar* and for their interest in the project; to Willis Barnstone for his reminiscence of the poet and for his support, suggestions, and encouragement in every phase of the work; and to my colleague, Ana María Douglas, who helped me with some of the most difficult phrases in Spanish.

Prologue by the Poet

The publication of these poems in English raises in my mind certain inevitable questions. Is there an audience for them? Who will that audience be? What will it be like? Poetic audience is without doubt the most difficult of all reading audiences to define in terms of vision and imagination, and one of the most difficult to visualize. The audience for poetry is a world of phantoms.

The playwright has the privilege of seeing his audience with his own eyes. It is right there before him for a few hours, inside the four walls of the theater. He can examine with his eyes the hundreds of different faces that make up the audience, take apart that complex and indistinct totality the way he might take a clock apart and examine all its tiny components one by one. He can say to himself: "The audience is that blond girl with her boyfriend, that corpulent gentleman who is half asleep, that slender, melancholy young fellow." As the playwright looks around the whole theater, the public materializes for him, defines itself, becomes—in a manner that is almost brutal—real and concrete.

The novelist, for his part, cannot bring his readers together in one place, nor can he study their individual faces. Nevertheless, he can have an idea of who constitutes his audience. How? From its beginnings, the novel has been a form of entertainment. In the Middle Ages, knights had enemies of flesh and blood. What greater sport could there be than fighting each other? But the ladies, in their castles, faced a truly terrifying enemy: time. They had to find something to do in their idleness: they had to kill time. The novel was a marvelous weapon in the battle to conquer the hours. In spite of everything that has been added to the vast pattern of the novel, the form maintains its character of pastime, of diversion. Therefore the audience of the novel is easier to find. It can be assumed that inside every reader of novels there is someone seeking entertainment, so the readership is vast: since almost everyone in our day and age seeks distraction, almost everyone can be included in the audience for the novel.

Novels and plays have one thing in common. They both aspire to distract us, to take us out of ourselves, to turn us into characters invented by the author. Novels and plays adapt themselves to the personalities of Tom, Dick, and Mary, or of Hamlet or Julien Sorrel, not to ours. We stop living with our own feelings in order to live inside those of another person that the author has invented to distract us, to transport us to a place where we will forget ourselves and take pleasure in the enchantment of being spectators.

But does poetry distract? That is highly doubtful. Instead of dis-tracting or at-tracting us to another place, poetry turns us inward, invites us to an interior activity, asks us to reproduce in our own hearts what the poet is feeling. Although a poem may be in essence a spiritual experience lived by the poet, that experience can be relived in the soul of the reader who reads deeply. It brings us face to face with ourselves, not with a character from a book or a play. It reaches down to the deep waters of our inner world, stirring and agitating them, always disrupting their calm. Like those people we love merely because they exist, a true poem attracts our deepest interest, makes us part of its life, makes us want to live in it. Only a certain kind of icy, indifferent professor or student can be a spectator of poetry, because poetry, like love, either conquers or ceases to exist. That is why poetry inspires a kind of fear: because instead of dis-tracting us, it re-tracts us, it draws us inward, into our own being. And what most people want now is to get outside of themselves, not to enter into themselves. The great malady of modern man is his incompatibility with his deepest, most mysterious self, which frightens him and produces in him an unconscious desire to escape. For that reason, he looks for all kinds of ways out of himself through the distractions that today's world provides him in abundance: dancing, sports, social life. Thus, our possible audience for poetry will be limited. It will be made up of those individuals who row against the current, who want to re-tract themselves, not dis-tract themselves, those people who want to look inward instead of outward. Reading poetry is not a simple endeavor: it requires an intense collaboration. How then can there be many readers of poetry in a world such as ours where people are so tired out by the pressures of work? Humanity has learned to look for opportunities to relax and not to participate, which is what one has to do in order to read a poem. We conclude, therefore, that the audience for poetry is sparse and distinguished. It is made up of individuals scattered everywhere. If an audience is an assembly, a gathering of people, a crowd, then poetry has no audience. It is not an aggregate; it is one plus one plus one, and so on.

No matter how much the general literary audience grows, I doubt that the audience of poetry lovers will grow proportionately. America, for example, offers the most extraordinary case of audiences ever known. The number of publications and sales is astonishing. They amaze me and frighten me, as the towers of Babylonia must have amazed and frightened people. They are one of the most prominent signs of the imperial magnitude of the United States. But, can we believe that this multiplication of readers, this fabulous business of our time, has affected the reader of poetry? I doubt it. Some poets complain about this; I find it a wonderful thing. With the exception of books by rhetorical or narrative poets, or poets of a nationalist stripe like Kipling, a book of poems has scant commercial value, the best efforts of marketing and advertising notwithstanding. It is impossible to popularize poetry, for the simple reason that poetry is not something of everyday use. This can be proved by the simple argument that few people of a certain class can go a whole year without reading a novel or going to the theater, while millions of people of that same social class live their whole lives without reading a book of poems.

Poetry is not for everyone. It is not the choice or caprice of poets that makes this so, and my argument should not be taken as a conceited declaration of aristocracy: on the contrary, it is the acceptance of a human truth, of a reality. Poets do not set out to write for the few, poetry simply *is* for the few. I suspect that all attempts to popularize it, to bring it beyond its natural boundaries, are false and artificial. Poetry has always been surrounded by an atmosphere of wonderment, and its power derives from that. Nothing protects it so much as its being an article of luxury, something useless and yet of exceptional value. How exciting and ironic it is to find the daily poem inside the *New York Times*! It is one of the most subtle things that can be pointed out to a foreigner in this city of relentless geometry. A friend of mine was complaining of the tiny space dedicated to poetry, in relation to the financial or sports sections, in the best newspaper in the world. It seems to me, on the contrary, an exquisite example of proportion. Like all things rare and precious, poetry cannot be measured by the usual standards. It is incomparable, in and of itself. That faithful and modest corner of the *New York Times* is the best evidence that poetry is invincible, precisely because its existence hardly requires any material space. And the daily, delicate, and inevitable presence of a poem under the protection of that magnificent publication is for me the perfect symbol of the place that poetry occupies and should occupy: barely visible, either subterranean or celestial, but always in the center of things, surrounded by the confusion of the fleeting signs and shadows that we call "daily news." If we think of life's goals in the way most of our contemporaries do, poetry is useless. It does not serve to teach or to distract us. Hence its place, more puzzling and more secure all the time, in the modern world. We move about in a world possessed by a manic desire for usefulness and efficiency. Man has peopled the earth with images of gods, in the image and likeness of his desires and dreams: machines. And in the commercial, functional world, poetry is transformed into something inexplicable, without place in the context of utilitarian activities. Poetry is superfluous, expendable, because for the great majority of people it does not contribute to the performance of any useful service.

It is for these reasons that in our civilization, grounded in technical capacities, social and economic sciences, and statistics, people find about as much justification for poetry as they do for palmistry. These days, poetry is in the air. It has no other place, which is fortunate, since air is its proper and natural element. Like the bird, it lives by the grace of liberty and the spirit of adventure. It is useless to try to turn it into a domesticated fowl—subjugated, confined, ready to be served at any time as everyday fare on the table. It won't abide cages or coops. And when the world seems to move toward lifestyles that resemble cages and coops, at first glance the fate of poetry would appear to be more endangered than ever. But that is not the case. Its salvation lies in its own resistance to all usefulness. The air is where poetry is safest. In that element it will live forever, while people go on working, calculating, and amusing themselves.

I began by asking where the audience for poetry might be found. Perhaps the answer is that the audience for poetry, like poetry itself, is everywhere and in no specific place, vast, innumerable, inapprehensible, but existent and inexplicable, like poetry.

To you, my audience of American readers, invisible, indeterminate, scattered in parts unknown, I offer my poems, like dice thrown to try my luck in the hands of those who still know how to read, in solitude, by the light of a lamp, a book of poems.

Prólogo del poeta

La aparición de algunos de mis poemas en inglés me plantea una pregunta inevitable. ¿Existe un público para estos poemas? ¿Quién será? ¿Cómo será? Me enfrento con un complicado tema de meditación: el problema del "público de la poesía". Sin duda, es el público cuya visión o cuya imaginación es más difícil de captar, y uno de los más difíciles de visualizar. Es un mundo fantasmagórico.

El dramaturgo tiene el privilegio de ver a su público con sus propios ojos. Ahí está ante él, durante unas horas, entre las cuatro paredes del teatro. Puede recorrer con sus ojos los cientos de rostros diversos que componen su público, deshacer ese todo complejo e indistinto, como desarmaría un reloj en sus diminutos componentes, y examinar una por una las partes del todo. Puede decirse: "El público es esa muchacha rubia con su novio, ese señor medio dormido y corpulento, ese joven esbelto y melancólico." Y así, pasando la vista por todo el teatro, el público se materializa para el dramaturgo, se define, se concretiza en forma casi brutal.

El novelista, por su parte, no puede, como el dramaturgo, reunir a sus lectores en un lugar definido, ni escrutar sus rostros individuales. Sin embargo, puede tener idea de quiénes constituyen su público. ¿Cómo? Desde sus comienzos, la novela fue una forma de entretenimiento. En la Edad Media, los caballeros tenían enemigos de carne y hueso. ¡Qué mayor diversión que esa especie de cacería humana! Pero las damas, en sus castillos, se enfrentaban con un terrible enemigo: el tiempo. Había que llenar los momentos de inacción: había que matar el tiempo. La novela era un maravilloso recurso en esta necesaria conquista de las horas. A pesar de todo lo que se le ha añadido al vasto patrón de la novela, dicha forma conserva su carácter de pasatiempo, de divertimento. Y por esa razón el público de la novela es más fácil de encontrar: se puede suponer que tras cada lector de novelas hay alguien que busca entretenerse; por lo tanto, el público de la novela es muy vasto: hoy en día, casi todo el mundo busca distracción, y por lo tanto, el público de la novela lo compone casi todo el mundo.

Las novelas y las obras de teatro tienen un punto de contacto. Ambas aspiran a distraernos, a sacarnos de nosotros mismos, a hacernos personajes inventados por el autor. La novela y el teatro no se ajustan a nuestras personas, sino a las de fulano o zutano, Hamlet o Julien Sorrel. Dejamos de vivir con nuestros sentimientos propios para vivir en los del vecino que ha inventado el autor para distaernos, para transportarnos allí donde nos olvidemos de nosotros mismos y tomemos gusto en el encanto de ser espectador.

Pero, ¿distrae la poesía? Eso es muy dudoso. Porque, en lugar de dis-traernos o a-traernos hacia otro lugar, nos hace volvernos hacia dentro, nos invita a una actividad interior, a algo así como reproducir en nuestro fuero interno lo que siente el poeta. Aunque un poema sea primordialmente una vivencia espiritual de la vida misma del poeta, si se lee como es debido, supone un revivir de esa experiencia en el alma del lector. Nos enfrenta con nosotros mismos, no con el personaje de un libro o de una obra de teatro. Alcanza a las aguas profundas del mundo interior, las toca y las agita, rompiendo siempre su sosiego. Como las gentes que, sólo por el hecho de existir, se hacen querer, un poema verdadero atrae nuestro interés más profundo, nos hace parte de su vivir, nos empuja al deseo de vivir en él. Sólo cierta clase de profesores y de alumnos frígidos pueden ser espectadores de la poesía; porque ésta, como el amor, o conquista o deja de existir. He aquí por qué la poesía inspira cierto miedo: porque en lugar de dis-traernos nos re-trae, nos aparta hacia dentro de nuestro ser. Y lo que casi todo el mundo desea hoy día es salir de sí, no entrar en sí. La gran enfermedad del hombre moderno es su incompatibilidad con su más profundo y misterioso yo, que le da miedo y le produce un deseo inconsciente de eludirlo. Por eso, se afana en toda suerte de salidas hacia lo externo, de distracciones que el mundo actual le provee en gran número: el baile, los deportes, la vida de sociedad. Y así, limitamos un poco nuestro posible público de poesía. Se compondrá de seres aparte, que van contra corriente, que quieren re-traerse, apartarse dentro de sí, no dis-traerse, que quieren mirar hacia dentro y no hacia el discurrir de fuera. La poesía no es simple lectura: requiere una intensa colaboración. Entonces,

¿cómo puede haber muchos lectores de poesía en un mundo como el de hoy, en el que tanto pesa el cansancio producido por el trabajo? La humanidad se ha acostumbrado a buscar pretextos para descansar y no para colaborar, que es lo que hay que hacer al leer un poema. Por lo tanto, deducimos que el público poético será escaso y distinguido. Se compone de individuos desparramados por todas partes. Si un público es una asamblea, una reunión de gente, una muchedumbre, la poesía no tiene público. No es un conglomerado; es uno más uno más uno, y así sucesivamente.

Por mucho que aumente el público literario general, no creo que el público amante de la poesía crezca en la misma proporción. Por ejemplo, América ofrece el caso mas extraordinario de "públicos" que se conoce en la historia. El número de ediciones y ventas es asombroso. Me maravillan y me aterran, como debieron maravillar y aterrar las torres de Babilonia. Son uno de los signos más prodigiosos de la magnitud imperial de Estados Unidos. Pero, ¿se puede creer que esa multiplicación del lector, esa empresa fabulosa de nuestro tiempo, haya alcanzado al lector de poesía? No lo creo. Algunos poetas se quejan de esto; a mí me parece excelente. A excepción de los libros de poetas elocuentes o narrativos, o de poetas de traza nacionalista, como Kipling, el libro de poemas es de poco valor mercantil, a pesar de los esfuerzos de la propaganda y el anuncio. Es imposible popularizar la poesía, por la simple razón de que no es un artículo de uso diario. Esto lo prueba el simple razonamiento de que pocas personas de cierta clase pueden vivir, pueden pasar un año sin leer una novela o ir al teatro, mientras que millones de seres de la misma clase social viven toda la vida sin haber leído un libro de versos. La poesía no es para todos, y esto no por elección ni capricho de los poetas. Y estas palabras no deben tomarse como una afirmación presuntuosa de aristocraticismo: por lo contrario, se trata de la aceptación de una verdad humana, de una realidad. No es que los poetas se propongan escribir para los pocos, no: es que la poesía *es* para los pocos. Sospecho que todo intento de popularizarla, de hacerla llegar más allá de sus límites naturales, es falso y artificial. La poesía siempre se ha rodeado de un ambiente de prodigio, y en ello reside su fuerza. Nada la protege tanto como el ser un artículo de lujo, algo sin utilidad, pero de valor excepcional. ¡Qué deliciosa e irónica emoción, la de la aparición del poema diario del *New York Times*! Es una de las cosas más delicadas que se le puedan señalar a un extranjero, en esa ciudad de implacable geometría. Un amigo mío se quejaba del poco espacio que se consagra, en relación con la sección financiera o de deportes, a la poesía en el mejor periódico del mundo. A mí, por el contrario, me parece un exquisito ejemplo de proporción. Como todas las cosas raras y preciosas, la poesía no se puede medir por normas usuales. Es algo incomparable, en sí. Ese fiel y modesto rincón del *New York Times* es el mejor testigo de que la poesía es invencible, precisamente porque su existencia apenas requiere espacio material. Y la diaria, delicada e inevitable presencia de un poema al secreto amparo de esa grandiosa publicación es para mí el perfecto símbolo del lugar que ocupa y debe ocupar la poesía: apenas visible, o subterránea o celestial, pero siempre en el centro rodeada por la confusión de los signos y sombras fugitivos que solemos llamar "noticias diarias". Si pensamos en las motivaciones de la vida tal y como las conciben la mayoría de nuestros contemporáneos, la poesía es inútil. Ni sirve para enseñar ni para distraer. De ahí el lugar que ocupa cada día, más desconcertante y más seguro a la vez, en el mundo moderno. Nos movemos en un mundo poseído por un ansia loca de utilidad y eficacia. El hombre ha poblado la tierra con imágenes de dioses, a imagen y semejanza de sus deseos y sus sueños: las máquinas. Y en el mundo mercantil y funcional, la poesía se transforma en algo inexplicable, sin lugar en el cuadro de actividades utilitarias. La poesía es superflua, está de más, porque para la gran masa de las gentes no contribuye a ninguna clase de servicio práctico.

   De ahí que en nuestra civilización, constituida por la capacidad técnica, por las ciencias sociales y económicas y por las estadísticas, las gentes encuentren tan poca justificación para la poesía como para la quiromancia. Hoy día, la poesía está en el aire. No le cabe otro lugar. Y eso, por fortuna, puesto que el aire es su elemento propio y natural. Como el ave, vive por gracia de la libertad y espíritu de aventura. Es inútil tratar de convertirla en un ave doméstica, subyugada, confinada, pronto a servir en cualquier momento, transformándose en el plato familiar de cada día. No admite jaulas ni corrales. Y cuando el mundo parece inclinarse hacia formas de vida que se asemejan más que nada a las jaulas y los corrales, a primera vista su sino parece peligrar más que nunca. Pero no es así. Su salvación reside en su misma resistencia a toda utilidad. El aire es donde está más segura. En ese elemento vivirá siempre, mientras las gentes trabajan, calculan o se divierten.

Por eso me preguntaba dónde se encuentra el público de la poesía. Quizá la respuesta sea que ese público está en todas partes y en ningún lugar determinado, como la misma poesía, que se trata de un público vasto, innumerable, inaprensible, pero existente e inexplicable, como la poesía.

A ustedes, lectores americanos, que no están ni aquí ni allí, les ofrezco estos poemas, como dados tirados al azar, para probar mi suerte en las manos de aquellos que sepan aún, en soledad, a la luz de la lámpara, leer un libro de versos.

A Life Because of Pedro Salinas

IN THE SUMMER OF 1947 I WAS IN GREEN MODEST VERMONT, AT THE Middlebury College Summer Language Program, where Pedro Salinas was the poet professor of the Spanish school. I had just come from Mexico, where I had spent some months in an Indian village near the great volcanoes south of the capital and the rest of the year in an orphanage in Mexico City for orphan children exiles from the Spanish Civil War (1936–1939). In those days the city had a large, active intellectual and artistic community of Spanish exiles who worked independently and at the universities. And from Spain came the mythical bullfighter Manolete to fight in the Mexican ring. Manolete, the lanky figure in Picasso's bullfighter lithograph who was to die shortly thereafter—gored in a provincial ring in Spain—transcended politics, war, and Franco. And then there was the traditional spring performance of José Zorrilla's *Don Juan Tenorio,* the Spanish Don Juan play. Spain in exile was alive in Mexico, which welcomed republican refugees.

During that winter and spring in the orphanage I lived in a small white room on the roof with a Catalán chemistry student, attended the University of Mexico, and taught English in the evenings to support myself. Since the Spanish orphanage gate was locked at ten, when I couldn't get back in time to get in or break in, I went to the apartment of Marti Franco, my recently widowed stepmother, who lived in an ancient slum barrio behind the cathedral. There I slept on the floor, on a mat between the Indian servant and Marti's brother Sam, a captain in the Mexican army. Marti's mother, Rebeca, a Spanish Jew from Constantinople, spoke to me in Ladino, the medieval Spanish of East European Jews. So, with all these diversities of Spanish language and cultural life behind me, I suddenly found myself at a pastoral retreat in New England which had seasonally attracted the great mafia of exiled scholars and poets from Spain, who were enriching college and university life in America.

Pedro Salinas was the star of the summer's program. Another in the Middlebury galaxy was Tomás Navarro Tomás, Spain's foremost linguist and Librarian of Spain. In the last terrible days of the civil war, Tomás had fled Spain in a military ambulance, accompanying the poet Antonio Machado, who was to die a month later in Collioure. One evening, Pedro Salinas gave a major lecture on the legendary Generation of 1927, a group of writers that included Federico García Lorca, Vicente Aleixandre (Noble laureate), Rafael Alberti, Luis Cernuda and Jorge Guillén. At a small reception following Salinas's talk, three poets of the '27 Generation were present: Luis Cernuda who had come up from Mount Holyoke, Jorge Guillén from Wellesley, and Salinas himself from John Hopkins. In the collected works of Lorca or Aleixandre are imperfect street snapshots of the '27 poets. One familiar one is of Lorca, Salinas, and Alberti, with Salinas in the center, wearing his habitual black fedora hat. Here in Vermont were survivors of that war and exile, three giants among twentieth-century European poets, standing together in a living picture, and close to all of us in that room.

In his writings on the Generation, Salinas elaborated a notion of friendship that was at the heart of this generation of Spanish poets, a generation representing the most significant rebirth of poetry in Spain in three hundred years. The gang of talented friends held together, and somehow their solidarity contributed to their fire, experimentation, individual genius, and optimism. In their vision they saw no less than a reformation of nation and culture. This enthusiasm of literary energy coincided with a similar resurgence in Spanish music, painting, and philosophy, yielding Casals, Segovia, Falla, Albéniz, Picasso, Gris, Dalí, Miró, Ortega, and Unamuno. However, the spirit of collaborative friendship emanating from '27 authors contrasted amusingly with the combative ways of the baroque poet Luis de Góngora (1563–1627) after whom the Generation of 1927 actually was named. (The year 1927 marked the tricentenary of Góngora's death.) Luis de Góngora and his contemporary Francisco de Quevedo insulted each other outrageously in their poems, giving another vitality to these last major voices of Spain's Golden Age.

I came to know Salinas through his lectures and poetry, but that summer I found myself in the Salinas history by the chance that Jaime Salinas, the poet's son, became my close friend and has remained so for decades. In the evenings we walked the beautiful, extensive campus, sometimes till dawn, never sure whether we were in the village or the countryside. And Jaime spoke about his father. He was proud not to have read his father's poems, yet he knew the poems intimately since when his father wrote a poem he read it to his son, either at home or when they were out walking togther. His father read him the poem and also told how the poem came to him.

In the early fall of 1947, Jaime invited me to spend a week at his house in Baltimore. There, each evening after supper, Pedro Salinas sat in his leather chair by the fireplace, we to his right on the couch. What took place was a *tertulia*, a special Spanish custom of literary conversation carried on at a café; but now the place of intimacy was the poet's living room. Don Pedro spoke in Spanish, and though he knew French well and enough English to defend himself, he knew he must preserve Spanish as his vital language in a sea of English speakers. He talked about the early Spanish epic *El cantar de mío Cid,* which he had edited and translated into modern verse; he also recalled his fellow poets, that family of writers he knew so well and who had formed each other. Some were dead. Miguel Hernández died in 1942 in a Spanish prison hospital, Lorca was executed outside his Granada in 1936, and Unamuno died in his sleep on December 31, 1936, while under house arrest after denouncing Franco and his generals at the University of Salamanca where he had been rector. One poet stayed on in Spain, Vicente Aleixandre, bedridden and unable to leave Madrid. He remained to nurture later generations of Spanish poets. The other poets were in exile—Alberti down in Argentina, Cernuda at Mount Holyoke but soon to return to Mexico, Juan Ramón Jiménez (Nobel laureate along with Aleixandre) in extended exile in Puerto Rico. The flowering of Spain was dispersed through death or exile. Although the center in Spain had collapsed, the survivors continued to write and were to compose abroad many of their most significant works.

In meeting Jaime and his father, I also met his wife, daughter, and son-in-law. Solita Salinas and Juan Marichal are still among my closest friends. But in those days, more than a half-century ago, one incident occurred on one of our noctural wanderings at Middlebury that was to affect every day of my life thereafter. And I hold the whole family guilty of contributing to this event. Their role in the incident included the ambience of Spanish literati which they personified, my sudden entry into Spanish poetry that they made possible, and the poet himself Salinas, who was astonishing for his literary fun, his avant-garde daring, his profound entanglement in Spanish tradition, and the fluency of his poems, which have at once the conversational plainness of the great Tang poets Li Bai, Du Fu, and Wang Wei and the confessional authority of later European and American poets. The family gave me example, but Jaime was the singular culprit.

While we were talking, and a crazy yellow moon had just come up in the predawn sky, after Jaime was declaiming great truths about Spain, about his childhood in Algeria, about the difficulties of being the son of a foremost poet of Spain, Jaime said to me, *Willis, en tu caso es distinto, porque eres poeta*—"Willis, in your case it's different, because you're a poet." "What do you mean, Jaime? I've never written a poem in my life," I protested. But he was right. In my case it was at least to be different. His words sank in. I soon received a copy from him of Rilke's *Letters to a Young Poet*. And six months later (by then I was twenty and a senior at Bowdoin College), I woke up in the middle of the night, wrote two poems. Next morning, I showed my things to my serious European student friends, a Frenchman, a Dane, and a Czech, all older and more mature because of the war, and these young intellectuals declared me a poet. I had the impudence to believe them, and after that never let up. I have not analyzed how Jaime came upon his declaration of my profession, but he inserted the seed, he incited the whole mess, at first in the unconscious or below it. On hearing my other European friends ordain me, I accepted the vice of poetry. I'm in debt to my Bowdoin friends and to the Salinas brood.

Pedro Salinas stayed on at Johns Hopkins, but just three years later he died of cancer, at age sixty, in a Boston hospital. I was then living in Greece, but had all my Spanish poet books with me. At this moment, after having outlived the beloved Don Pedro and having just published *Algebra of Night: New and Selected 1948–1998*, I do not know if I would have written any of these poems had I not had the amazing luck of finding myself in the midst of that Salinas family, whose father was the model and son the conspirator.

I thank them all with love and nostalgia.

A LIFE BECAUSE OF PEDRO SALINAS

* * *

That gracious and profound poet Pedros Salinas, one of the century's signifying modernists, was the architect of innovation in Spain, the dean of poet critics, and a mesmerizing teacher. One of his books I later translated, *La voz a ti debida* (*My Voice Because of You*), a powerful sequence of related poems. Among the books in this genre of linked poems in Europe, Salinas's *My Voice,* together with Rilke's *Sonnets to Orpheus* and Lorca's *Gypsy Balladbook,* seems to me one of the enduring and most precious books the world has given us. Salinas's sequence is an extraordinary love poem of subtlety, breadth of language, pathos, beauty, and impossibility.

My Voice follows Salinas's trilogy of early books, of which *Seguro azar* (*Certain Chance*), here brilliantly translated by David Lee Garrison, carries all the vitality and diversity of this grand metaphysical poet. Dazzlingly modern, in common speech, he sees lovers, spark plugs, clouds, and electric princesses in light bulbs as all part of a contiguous landscape and psyche. As Blake discovered his city of doomed children, chimney sweeps, and satanic mills, Salinas found another city where new technology is an enticing passage of the soul. Garrison has made this gem in the Salinas collection a marvelous poem in English. In it Salinas, like an old Kabbalist, counts the stars in his alphabet book. We are in debt to Garrison for giving us Salinas's constellation of poems, which appears naked on islands of horizontality.

Willis Barnstone
Bloomington, Indiana
June 1999

Translator's Introduction

PEDRO SALINAS (1891–1951) WAS BORN IN MADRID AND RECEIVED HIS doctorate in Spanish literature at the University of Madrid in 1917. After teaching at Cambridge, the Sorbonne, and the universities of Seville and Murcia, he returned to his home city as a professor at the University of Madrid. He was one of a great generation of poets that included Federico García Lorca, Vicente Aleixandre (Nobel Prize, 1977), Rafael Alberti, and Jorge Guillén, among many others. Almost all these men died or were forced into exile during the Spanish Civil War (1936–1939). Salinas came to the United States in 1938 and taught at Wellesley, Bryn Mawr, Johns Hopkins, and Middlebury. He published one collection of short stories and another of plays, a novel, seven volumes of essays and literary criticism, and nine books of poetry. He wrote *Seguro azar* (*Certain Chance*) between 1924 and 1928, and it was published for the first time in 1929.

The title *Seguro azar* exemplifies the rich ambiguity of Salinas's poetry. It is an oxymoron that is hard to translate mainly because there is no English word that reflects with precision the Spanish word *azar*. It can mean "chance" or "luck," and in this sense it forms part of the phrase *al azar*, which is often used to describe the kind of random luck involved in a game of chance. It can also stand for the great gamble of life itself—"fate" or "destiny"—and it can indicate "bad luck," "unforeseen disaster," "accident," "risk," or "danger." It often suggests some combination of these meanings simultaneously. The adjective that modifies *azar* in Salinas's title, *seguro,* adds another level of ambiguity, for it implies that somehow random luck is certain, or that destiny, danger, or disaster are certain, or that any one or all of these things are safe and secure.

If we look to the poems to unravel the enigmatic title, we only find more ambiguity, for Salinas undermines the stability we attach to linguistic signs and everyday realities. In his poetry, words and things are never what we expect them to be. Salinas subverts our expectations when he describes things we think we know—a piece of paper, a darkened room, a tree, a shoreline—in such a way that we often do not recognize them at first. His take on these things is sometimes whimsical, as in "35 bujías" (35 Candle Power), in which he refers to a lightbulb as "my artificial princess / my electric lover." It is sometimes sad, as in "El árbol menos" (The Missing Tree), where he describes the sense of meaninglessness caused when a field is left empty by the cutting down of a cypress tree. It is often self-conscious, as in "Cuartilla" (Page), the opening poem, which describes a snowy winter landscape wherein everything is white, including, as the poet suggests through the title and the last line, the blank page on which he composes. The snowscape becomes a metaphor that represents the white space where the poet's imagination takes shape. Salinas first draws us into the scene by causing us to imagine the reality of a winter scene, then reveals that scene as an abstraction representing the place where printed words create imaginary worlds.

"Cuartilla" is one of many poems in the collection that point to the act of literary creation. "Soledades de la obra" (Solitudes of Creation), for example, has to do with the poet's changing feelings toward a poem during and after the act of writing it, and "Quietud" (Peacefulness) deals with the necessary place of idleness in the creative process. The final poem, "Su triunfo" (His Triumph), is about finishing a book, just as the first one is about starting one. The last line of "Su triunfo" has a tripartite structure that echoes the last line of "Cuartilla," yet the tone of the two poems is radically different. While the first one expresses the joy of getting the first word down, the last one strikes out in anger at silence, at the inevitable silence that follows a poem, a book, a life. The act of writing is seen in the end as a struggle, a losing battle against the silence of eternity.

Seguro azar is a kind of dialogue in which the poet speaks to things and people as he searches for their true essence. The result of this search is a vision of the world that constantly surprises us with its unusual perspective. In "Navacerrada, abril" (Navacerrada, April), a man stops his car in a mountain pass (Navacerrada) to look at the valley below him, then goes on to describe his much more immediate environment—the car in which he is traveling. He personifies the car as his friend, as his fellow adventurer, as the "mechanical soul" in which his own soul is temporarily housed. He lends human characteristics to the car and talks to it throughout the poem, and yet at the same time he delights in its technology, in its mechanical existence. Curiously, the focus of the poem moves away from the subject announced in the title—a mountain pass in April—to the car that travels through that place and season. The whimsy of this vantage point reveals a joy in observing not only the landscape a traveler would ordinarily observe, but also the technological wonder that allows him to observe it.

In another poem involving car travel, "Aviso" (Warning), the poet portrays the always imminent menace involved in driving. The speaker is speeding along when suddenly death appears, not in its traditional guise as "skeleton" or "symbol," but as something "tall, erect, blinding, / serious as the letter 'I.' " All at once, the speaker / driver sees only lines and letters: the letter "I" (a wall he might crash into?), "white stripes / on a black background" (center stripes on the highway?) and then three other letters (from a billboard or a license plate?). His life is threatened by the lines on the black background and the lines that create the letters, then saved by the lines of "a triangle: / the brake against all four wheels." Throughout this poem—indeed, throughout the collection—Salinas's poetry ebbs and flows with a kind of delirious free association that suggests deeply instinctual or unconscious things. At the climactic moment of "Aviso," for example, Salinas delays the narrative in order to repeat the key verb in different tenses: "struck, will strike, strikes, would strike!" While this may at first seem to be an illogical digression, it is in fact a powerful way of suggesting the speaker's experience of peril, his altered sense of time in a sudden crisis. It is as though the terrified speaker/driver is asking himself, in a split second that seems like an hour, if death struck, if it is striking, if it will or would strike. Offering these different time frames for the action brings us into the poem by suggesting the panic and disorientation of the driver. Poetic techniques such as this create a kind of dialogue between us and the poet as we follow the different paths of meaning that he points out.

The unusual perspectives Salinas creates help him suggest ambiguous dimensions of human interaction and existence. "Otra tú" (Another You), for example, examines our traditional understanding of dialogue. The "I" in the poem sees "you" only through the water, hears "you" only through silence, communicates with "you" only through the medium of elements within the natural world. The whole poem reflects the indirect nature of communication, which takes place largely through the ambiguous, multivalent abstractions of spoken or written language. Just as the speaker in "Another You" communicates indirectly through the world around him, so all human beings communicate indirectly through the medium of language.

The "you" in "Another You" is a woman—this is made clear by the feminine adjective in the Spanish title, "Otra tú"—and she appears in many other poems in the collection, always in contexts that suggest an intimacy with the speaker. And yet few of these are what we might think of as traditional love poems expressing praise or appreciation. More often, they suggest the complexities and strange difficulties of love. In fact, in some poems the speaker or his lover is angry, or both people are angry. In "Sin voz, desnuda" (Without Voice, Naked), for example, the woman has wrapped herself in silence, and communication is impossible. She seems strangely vulnerable, as suggested by the title word *desnuda* (naked); yet her silence girds and protects her. The speaker, unable to talk with her, warns that "the blade of silence you are sharpening . . . will kill you." In a much happier poem, "Dominio" (Dominion), the speaker admires the strange power of the woman to link night and day for him through one word—*adiós*.

Physical intimacy or presence is often not true intimacy in the love poems of *Seguro azar*. Salinas looks for love's deeper essences and implies that finding real connection with another person is often an elusive, labyrinthine process. In the strange poem "Sí reciente" (Recent Yes), the speaker says, "Love, I do not love you very much." It is not clear whether he is talking to his lover or to love itself, but it is very clear that he is saying that presence—the togetherness of lovers—can actually obscure the true awareness of love, that memory can offer a better understanding of it. If poetry is "powerful emotions recollected in tranquility," as Wordsworth wrote, love can sometimes be best comprehended through recollection. Paradoxically, in this and other poems, separation from his lover allows the speaker a deeper understanding of her and of their relationship. *Seguro azar* is a kind of rediscovery of the world that Salinas achieves through his radical vision of everyday realities and through his consummate skill in making "constant tiny erosions in grammar, in conventional usage, in the reigning norms of language."[1] The philosopher José Ortega y Gasset used those words to define creativity, arguing that a translator has to re-create those erosions in order to express the life of the original text. The ambiguous language and syntax, the elliptical quality, the openness of Salinas's poems has made them the greatest translating challenge I have ever encountered. Bringing his creative erosions into English, finding ways to reveal his originality without sacrificing intelligibility, has forced me to make difficult decisions in every poem, sometimes in every line. I have tried throughout the book to achieve what I consider the essential goal of translation—the creation of poems that do not simply reflect the original texts but exist as viable and vital poems in English. Unless a translation thrives in its new linguistic context, unless it is a poem in its own right, it remains stuck in a limbo between the two languages as "translationese."

The last few lines of "Cuartilla" provide a good example of the kinds of problems I have had to solve:

> *Pero el viento desata*
> *deserciones, huidas.*
> *Y la que vence es*
> *rosa, azul, sol, el alba:*
> *punta de acero, pluma*
> *contra lo blanco, en blanco,*
> *inicial, tú, palabra.*

Literally, this means:

> But the wind unleashes
> desertions, escapes.
> And the winner is
> rose, blue, sun, the dawn:
> steel point, feather
> against the white, in/on white,
> first, you, word.

My translation is:

> But the wind unleashes
> to allow desertions, escapes,
> and victory for
> rose, blue, sun, dawn:
> a steel point, a feather
> against the whiteness of a blank
> page, you, first word.

In my second line I have had to add the infinitive "to allow," which is only implicit in the Spanish, for three reasons: (1) to clarify the passage, (2) to merge the first two lines into a more fluid whole, and (3) to avoid a line that sounds like the climax of a thousand television game shows in English—"And the winner is. . . ."

The word *pluma* presents another difficulty because in Spanish it can mean both "feather" and "pen." Since the image of the "steel point" in this context clearly suggests a pen, I have decided to use "feather" at the end of the line to preserve that connotation as well. The last two lines also include a word with a double meaning—*blanco* can mean both "white" and "blank." Since the title and the context suggest the idea of writing, and because the phrase "en blanco" often refers to the blankness of a page, I decided to clarify these implications by using the word *page* in my translation even though it does not appear in the Spanish text.

In the final line, Salinas separates the adjective *inicial* from the noun it modifies in order to end the poem with a dramatic series of three words, each one followed by a comma that creates a dramatic pause. This separation also reverses the normal word order, giving the line a kind of biblical effect that recalls the opening hyperbaton from John's Gospel ("In the beginning was the Word . . .") and causing the adjective *inicial* to modify both *tú* (you) and *palabra* (word) instead of just *palabra*. I wanted to respect this rhetorical arrangement of the words and salvage the meaning that is lost in the literal translation. To do this, I placed "page" in the last line to create the pauses and the tripartite division in the Spanish, while keeping the adjective and noun together for the sake of clarity in the final lines, thus: "a feather / against the whiteness of a blank / page, you, first word."

As a translator, I have had to face the same white page Salinas did, yet within that page I have had his Spanish words to follow like footsteps in the snow. I have followed his lead, and I hope that, like his pen, mine has had its share of victories.

Note

1. "Escribir bien consiste en hacer continuamente pequeñas erosiones a la gramática, al uso establecido, a la norma vigente de la lengua." José Ortega y Gasset, "Miseria y esplendor de la traducción," *Obras completas* (Madrid: Revista de Occidente, 1947) 5:429–48 (at p. 430).

Woods Study #1. 1992. 5 × 6 in., intaglio.

Certain Chance

Seguro Azar

1

Cuartilla

Invierno, mundo en blanco.
Mármoles, nieves, plumas,
blancos llueven, erigen
blancura, a blanco juegan.
Ligerísimas,
escurridizas, altas,
las columnas sostienen
techos de nubes blancas.
Bandas
de palomas dudosas entre blancos, arriba
y abajo, vacilantes
aplazan
la suma de sus alas.
¿Vencer, quién vencerá?
Los copos inician algaradas.
Sin ruido choques, nieves,
armiños, encontrados.
Pero el viento desata
deserciones, huidas.
Y la que vence es
rosa, azul, sol, el alba:
punta de acero, pluma
contra lo blanco, en blanco,
inicial, tú, palabra.

1

Page

Winter, world in white.
Marble, snow, feathers
rain shades of white, pile up
whiteness, play in white.
Lithe,
slippery, tall,
the columns hold up
roofs of white clouds.
Flocks
of doves vacillate between whites above
and below,
holding back
the full force of their wings.
Win, who is going to win?
Snowflakes launch surprise attacks.
Noiseless collisions, snows,
ermines, discovered.
But the wind unleashes
to allow desertions, escapes,
and victory for
rose, blue, sun, dawn:
a steel point, a feather
against the whiteness of a blank
page, you, first word.

2

Figuraciones

Parecen nubes. Veleras,
voladoras, lino, pluma,
al viento, al mar, a las ondas
—parecen el mar—del viento,
al nido, al puerto, horizontes,
certeras van como nubes.

Parecen rumbos. Taimados
los aires soplan al sesgo,
el sur equivoca al norte,
alas, quillas, trazan rayas,
—aire, nada, espuma, nada—,
sin dondes. Parecen rumbos.

Parece el azar. Flotante
en brisas, olas, caprichos,
¡qué disimulado va,
tan seguro, a la deriva
querenciosa del engaño!
¡Qué desarraigado, ingrávido,
entre voces, entre imanes,
entre orillas, fuera, arriba,
suelto! Parece el azar.

2

Imaginings

They look like clouds. Swift-sailing,
flying—canvas and feather
in the wind, in the sea, in waves
of wind that look like the sea;
they skim, steady as clouds,
to the nest, to the port, to horizons.

They look like paths. Cunning
winds strike at a slant until
south is taken for north,
until wings and keels draw lines
—wind, nothing, foam, nothing—
to nowhere. They look like paths.

It looks like chance. Floating
on breezes, waves, caprices—
how surreptitiously, how surely
it moves with the home-loving
drift of illusion!
So uprooted and weightless
between voices, between magnets,
between shores, out there, up high,
free! It looks like chance.

3

Otra tú

No te veo la mirada
si te miro aquí a mi lado.
Si miro al agua la veo.

Si te escucho,
no te oigo bien el silencio.
En la tersura
del agua quieta lo entiendo.

Y el cielo
—tú le miras, yo le miro—,
no es infinito en lo alto:
el cielo
—en su baranda te apoyas—
tiene cuatro esquinas, húmedo,
está en el agua, cuadrado.

3

Another You

I don't see the look in your eyes
if I glance at you here beside me,
but I do if I look in the water.

If I listen to you
I hardly hear your silence,
but in the smoothness
of the still water I understand it.

And the sky
—you look at it, I look at it—
is not infinite up there:
the sky
—you lean against its railing—
has four corners, wet,
lies in the water, square.

4

Vocación

Abrir los ojos. Y ver
sin falta ni sobra, a colmo
en la luz clara del día
perfecto el mundo, completo.
Secretas medidas rigen
gracias sueltas, abandonos
fingidos, la nube aquella,
el pájaro volador,
la fuente, el tiemblo del chopo.
Está bien, mayo, sazón.
Todo en el fiel. Pero yo . . .
Tú, de sobra. A mirar,
y nada más que a mirar
la belleza rematada
que ya no te necesita.

Cerrar los ojos. Y ver
incompleto, tembloroso,
de será o de no será,
—masas torpes, planos sordos—
sin luz, sin gracia, sin orden
un mundo sin acabar,
necesitado, llamándome
a mí, o a ti, o a cualquiera
que ponga lo que le falta,
que le dé la perfección.

4

Vocation

To open my eyes and see
the world, wasting nor wanting nothing,
perfect and complete at its zenith
in the bright light of day.
Secret measures control
elegance run wild, feigned
desertions, that cloud over there,
that bird in flight,
the fountain, the poplar's tremor.
All is well—May, the season,
everything in balance. But I . . .
You are superfluous—here only
to look, nothing more,
to look at this climax of beauty
that no longer needs you.

To close my eyes and see,
imperfect and trembling,
something of what will or will not be,
—crude mounds, silent plains—
an endless world
without light, without charm, without order,
needy, calling out
to me, or to you, or to anyone
who can fill its need,
who can give it perfection.

En aquella tarde clara,
en aquel mundo sin tacha,
escogí:
      el otro.
Cerré los ojos.

On that bright afternoon
in that flawless world
I chose:
       the other world.
I closed my eyes.

5

Pasajero apresurado

Ciudad, ¿te he visto o no?
La noche era una prisa
por salir de la noche.
Tú al paso me ofreciste
gracias vagas, en vano.
Aquella catedral
que disparaba piedras
a la niebla . . . No sé
qué agua turbia, raptora
de luces a los puentes.
Inaccesibles entre
su guardia de cristales
perla, flor o pintura,
corazón de las tiendas.
Y hubo una pantorrilla
tersa en la media fina,
cuando el asfalto ofrece
sucio azogue a las nubes.

5

Hurried Traveler

City, did I see you or not?
That night was a rush
to leave the night.
In vain you offered me
a blur of elegance
as I passed through.
That cathedral
firing stones
into the fog . . . some
murky water pillaging
lights from the bridges.
Inaccessible between
guardians of glass
was the heart of each store—
pearl, flower, or painting.
And one smooth calf appeared
in sheer hose
when the asphalt offered
its muddy quicksilver to the clouds.

6

El zumo

¡Tan visible está el secreto!
¡Tan alegre,
tan alegre,
colgando al aire!
Le ven todas las miradas,
y le sopesan los vientos;
los chiquillos le conocen
y gritan: "Mira, un secreto.
¡Dámelo! Si parece una naranja."
Pero el secreto defiende,
invisible amarga almendra,
su mañana, su secreto
mayor, dentro.
Lo que da son disimulos,
redondez, color, rebrillo,
solución fácil, naranja,
a la mirada y al viento.

6

Juice

The secret is so visible!
Happy,
so happy,
hanging in the air!
All eyes see it
and the winds heft it;
little children know it
and shout: "Look, a secret.
Give it to me! It just looks like an orange."
But the secret protects—
invisible bitter almond—
its tomorrow, its biggest
secret, inside itself.
What it gives away are disguises,
roundness, color, luster,
the easy answer, an orange
to the eye and to the wind.

7

Sin voz, desnuda

Sin armas. Ni las dulces
sonrisas, ni las llamas
rápidas de la ira.
Sin armas. Ni las aguas
de la bondad sin fondo,
ni la perfidia, corvo pico.
Nada. Sin armas. Sola.
Ceñida en tu silencio.
"Si" y "no", "mañana" y "cuando"
quiebran agudas puntas
de inútiles saetas
en tu silencio liso
sin derrota ni gloria.
¡Cuidado! que te mata
—fría, invencible, eterna—
eso, lo que te guarda,
eso, lo que te salva,
el filo del silencio que tú aguzas.

7

Without Voice, Naked

Unarmed. No gentle
smiles, no sudden
flames of anger.
Unarmed. Not even
the bottomless waters of kindness
or the crooked beak of treachery.
Nothing. Unarmed. Alone.
Girded by your silence.
"Yes" and "no," "tomorrow" and "when"
break the sharp points
of their arrows in vain
against your smooth silence
without victory or defeat.
Careful! What is killing you
—cold, invincible, eternal—
is the same thing that protects you,
that saves you:
the blade of silence you are sharpening.

8

Fecha cualquiera

¡Ay qué tarde organizada
en surtidor y palmera
en cristal recto, desmayo
en palma curva, querencia!

Dos líneas se me echan
encima a campanillazos
paralelas del tranvía.
Pero yo quiero a esas otras
que se van
sin llevarme por el cielo:
telégrafo, nubes blancas,
y
—compás de los horizontes—
el pico de las cigüeñas.

¡Qué perfecto lo redondo
verde, azul! ¡Ay, si se suelta!
Lo tiene un niño de un hilo.
¡Quieto,
aire del sur, aire aire!
La pura geometría,
dime,
¿quién se la quita a la tarde?

8

Could Be Any Day

What an afternoon—drawn together
by a fountain and a palm tree,
a right angle of glass, a swoon
in the palm's curve, a deep longing!

Two lines throw themselves
on top of me with clanging bells:
streetcar tracks.
But I want those other lines
that disappear
without carrying me through the sky:
telegraph, white clouds,
and
—compass of horizons—
the stork's beak.

The green and blue globe
is so perfect. Watch out, it might slip free!
A child holds it by a thread.
Wind from the south,
be still, wind, wind.
Tell me,
who can take away the pure geometry
of this afternoon?

9

El mal invitado

Quedarme aquí
en esta casa
donde estoy de paso.
Y lo que cogen los ojos
con torpe prisa de avaro
—ángulo, relumbre en sombra,
hoja y cielo en la almohada—,
visto al fulgor del momento,
y lo agavillan ansiosos
para llevárselo,
verlo despacio,
a luz de sol y de luna,
a luz de estío y otoño,
a luz de goce y de pena.
Verlo tanto
que esto que me queda ahora
clavado e inolvidable
como el más alto cantar,
esto, que nunca se olvidará
en mí porque fue del tiempo,
de tan mío, de tan visto,
de tan descifrado, fuera,
eternidad, lo olvidado.

9

The Greedy Guest

I want to stay here
in this house
I am visiting.
My eyes take hold of things
with the clumsy haste of a miser
in this momentary glow
—angle, shadowy luster,
leaf and sky on the pillow—
and wrap them, eager
to take them away
and examine them slowly
by the light of sun and moon,
summer and fall,
pleasure and pain.
My eyes want to take everything in
so that what stays with me now,
fixed and unforgettable
as a lofty hymn,
what will never slip from my memory—
because it belonged to time,
because it was so much mine, so closely
examined and deciphered—will become
eternity, what is forgotten.

10

Navacerrada, abril

Los dos solos. ¡Qué bien
aquí, en el puerto, altos!
Vencido verde, triunfo
de los dos, al venir
queda un paisaje atrás:
otro enfrente, esperándonos.
Parar aquí un minuto.
Sus tres banderas blancas
—soledad, nieve, altura—
agita la mañana.
Se rinde, se me rinde.
Ya su silencio es mío:
posesión de un minuto.
Y de pronto mi mano
que te oprime, y tú, yo,
—aventura de arranque
eléctrico—, rompemos
el cristal de las doce,
a correr por un mundo
de asfalto y selva virgen.
Alma mía en la tuya
mecánica; mi fuerza,
bien medida, la tuya,
justa: doce caballos.

10

Navacerrada, April

Just the two of us. So good
to be up here in the mountain pass!
Together we have conquered the green,
arriving in triumph,
leaving one landscape behind:
another lies ahead, waiting for us.
Let's stop here a minute.
Morning is waving
its three white flags—
solitude, snow, elevation.
It surrenders, surrenders to me.
Its silence is mine
if only for a minute.
And suddenly my hand
holding you, you and I
—an adventure of electric
ignition—break
the glass of twelve
to run through a world
of asphalt and virgin forest.
My soul inside your
mechanical soul; my force
well-measured, yours
exact: twelve horses.

11

Orilla

¿Si no fuera por la rosa
frágil, de espuma, blanquísima,
que él, a lo lejos se inventa,
quién me iba a decir a mí
que se le movía el pecho
de respirar, que está vivo,
que tiene un ímpetu dentro,
que quiere la tierra entera,
azul, quieto, mar de julio?

11

Shore

Were it not for the fragile rose
of white, white foam
it invents in the distance,
who could have told me that the rising
and falling of its chest
was breathing, that it's alive,
that some inner force impels it,
that this calm blue ocean of July
desires the entire earth?

12

Tránsito

¡Qué princesa final—la última hoja
de otoño—pasa por en medio, lenta,
de la ancha calle sola!
Rubia, desheredada, morganática
esposa del gorrión. Presentan armas,
inútiles aceros, ramas secas,
dobles filas de árboles, la guardia.
¡Adiós!
Las encendidas iluminaciones
urbanas a su muerte paraísos
eléctricos ofrecen, blancos campos
elíseos. ¡Arriba!
El viento, su destino, ya la sube,
alma, al cielo.
¡Adiós! Invierno, ¡qué anarquía!, invierno.
Las dinastías verdes
cumpliendo trasatlánticos destierros,
esperan
abril, clarín, restauración segura.

12

Transition

The last princess—autumn's
last leaf—drifts down the middle
of the wide empty street.
Blond, disinherited, morganatic wife
of the sparrow. Double rows of trees
stand guard and present arms
with their useless swords: bare branches.
¡Adiós!
City lights go on,
offering her death in electric paradise,
in white Elysian fields. Upward!
Now the wind, her destiny, swoops her up,
soul and all, to the sky.
¡Adiós! Winter—what anarchy!—winter.
Green dynasties
in transatlantic exile
wait for
April, clarion, safe return.

13

Los equívocos

La tarde en sazón fija
a un otoño que escapa
tumultos apacigua.
Primeras nieves: blanco . . .
Horizontes: aquello . . .
Distancia vista es
lejanía medida.
Ni mar ni cielo engañan:
embusteros los dos.
Lo cierto en el columpio
vuelos de seda enseña.
El mundo es infinito,
profusión de mentira.
De verdad
recta y curva no más.
Geometría, nieve,
ingrávidas queridas.

13

Illusions

This afternoon—attached
by season to an escaping autumn—
calms the uproar.
First snows: whiteness . . .
Horizons: something over there . . .
Distance seen
is remoteness measured.
Neither sea nor sky can deceive,
both are impostors.
What is certain on the swing
reveals flights of silk.
The earth is infinite,
a profusion of lies.
No more truth,
straight or curved.
Geometry, snow,
weightless lovers.

Sparse Trees, Winter. 1995. 14 × 19 in., gouache on paper.

14

Quietud

No, si no se acaba hoy
esto que tengo empezado,
ya lo sé . . . Sí hay que dejarlo.
Tú, alfabeto, tú, intención,
tú, papel blanco, ¡qué inútiles
esta noche
que otra perfección me entrega,
infecunda virgen alta,
de cristal, antigua, inmóvil!
Me llama un ocio, un quehacer
de no hacer nada, de estarse
como agua pura, ni río,
ola ni torrente, agua
quieta esperando que pasen
por arriba alas o nubes,
las almas que tengo fuera.
Un ocio
tan hondo que yo ya sé
que lo que tengo empezado
se cumple en el no acabar,
su sinfín tiene perfecto.

14

Peacefulness

No, what I've begun
won't get finished today,
I know that . . . Yes, I've got to put it down.
You, letters, you, intentions,
you, blank page, you are all useless
tonight,
for another perfection has hold of me:
a tall glass virgin,
sterile, ancient, immovable.
Idleness calls me to the task
of doing nothing, of being
like pure water, neither river
nor wave nor torrent: quiet water
waiting for wings or clouds,
for the souls I have outside me
to pass over.
An idleness
so profound I know now
that what I've begun
will be finished by not finishing,
that its endlessness is perfect.

Table Study, 1983. 13¼ × 16 in., ink on paper.

15

Far West

¡Qué viento a ocho mil kilómetros!
¿No ves cómo vuela todo?
¿No ves los cabellos sueltos
de Mabel, la caballista
que entorna los ojos limpios
ella, viento, contra el viento?
¿No ves
la cortina estremecida,
ese papel revolado
y la soledad frustrada
entre ella y tú por el viento?

Sí, lo veo.
Y nada más que lo veo.
Ese viento
está al otro lado, está
en una tarde distante
de tierras que no pisé.
Agitando está unos ramos
sin dónde,
está besando unos labios
sin quién.
No es ya viento, es el retrato
de un viento que se murió
sin que yo le conociera,
y está enterrado en el ancho
cementerio de los aires
viejos, de los aires muertos.

15

Far West

A wind of eight thousand kilometers per hour!
Don't you see how everything flies?
Don't you see the windblown locks
of Mabel, the horseback rider
half-closing her clear eyes,
a wind against the wind?
Don't you see how the wind
billows the curtain,
sends that paper whirling,
foils the separation
between her and you?

Yes, I see it.
And that's all—I see it.
That wind
is on the other side, is
on a distant afternoon
in lands I've never been to.
It is stirring some branches
from nowhere,
kissing some lips,
but whose?
Now it isn't wind, it's the painting
of a wind that died
before I encountered it,
and it is buried in the vast
cemetery of old winds,
of dead winds.

Sí le veo, sin sentirle.
Está allí, en el mundo suyo,
viento de cine, ese viento.

Yes, I see it without feeling it.
That wind is there in its own world,
that wind of the cinema.

16

Dominio

Con tu palabra última
—adiós—
anoche encadenaste
la noche a tu silencio.
Aunque el rayo de sol
en los ojos me hiera
con su ciega evidencia,
la noche limpia y pura
tal como anoche era
en tu silencio se conserva.
Y no se irá a su nada,
secreta, ultraterrena,
hasta que tú, con la primera palabra
de tus labios de hoy
—adiós—crees el día.

16

Dominion

With your last word last night
—*adiós*—
you linked the night
to your silence.
Though the rays of the sun
wound my eyes
with their blind evidence,
the night—clean and pure
as last night was—
lingers in your silence
and cannot fade into its secret
otherworldly nothingness
until you, with the first word
from your lips, today's lips,
—*adiós*—create the day.

17

Los mares

El mar. Chasquido breve,
muerte de adolescencia
sobre la arena tibia.
Playa.

El mar. Ámbito exacto:
allí acaba, aquí empieza,
aquí estoy yo, allí ella.
Ausencia.

El mar. Embate plano
contra rocas tajadas.
Escribe blanca espuma
en el cantil su acróstico.
Se lo descifra el viento.
Secreto.

El mar. Sal en los labios
que beso, y esa gota
que va rodando, ajena,
por mejilla sin llanto.
La sal y el agua
en el amor y en el aire.

El mar. Las rastrojeras
ardidas.
Un chopo solo y quieto.
Esqueléticos galgos
buscan agua en un cauce
seco.

17

Oceans

The ocean. Sudden crack,
death of adolescence
on the warm sand.
Beach.

The ocean. Circumscribed exactly:
there it ends, here it begins,
here I am, there she is.
Absence.

The ocean. Slapping flat
against crags,
writing its acrostic
in white foam on the precipice.
Wind deciphers for the rock.
Secret.

The ocean. Salt on the lips
I kiss, and that teardrop
rolling, far away,
down a dry cheek.
Salt and water
on love and wind.

The ocean. Burned
stubble.
A poplar, still and solitary.
Skeletal greyhounds
sniff for water
in a parched riverbed.

18

Don de la materia

Entre la tiniebla densa
el mundo era negro: nada.
Cuando de un brusco tirón
—forma recta, curva forma—
le saca a vivir la llama.
Cristal, roble, iluminados
¡qué alegría de ser tienen,
en luz, en líneas, ser
en brillo y veta vivientes!
Cuando la llama se apaga
fugitivas realidades,
esa forma, aquel color,
se escapan.
¿Viven aquí o en la duda?
Sube lenta una nostalgia
no de luna, no de amor,
no de infinito. Nostalgia
de un jarrón sobre una mesa.
¿Están?
Yo busco por donde estaban.
Desbrozadora de sombras
tantea la mano. A oscuras
vagas huellas sigue el ansia.
De pronto, como una llama
sube una alegría altísima
de lo negro: luz del tacto.
Llegó al mundo de lo cierto.
Toca el cristal, frío, duro,
toca la madera, áspera.

18

The Gift of Matter

Amid dense shadows
the world was black: nothing,
when with an abrupt strike
—straight shape, curved shape—
the flame brings it to life.
Glass and oak glow—
what joy they have in being,
their vein and luster alive
in light and lines.
When the flame goes out,
fugitive realities—
that form, that color—
escape.
Do they live here or in doubt?
A deep longing rises,
not for the moon, not for love,
not for infinity. Longing
for a vase upon a table.
Are these things here?
I look at where they were.
Clearing away the shadows,
my hands grope for things. Desire
retraces vague steps
through the darkness.
Suddenly, joy
bursts like a flame
from the blackness: the light of touch
arrived in the world of certainty,
touching the cold hard glass,
following the rough grain of the wood.

¡Están!
La sorda vida perfecta
sin color, se me confirma,
sugura, sin luz, la siento:
realidad profunda, masa.

They're here!
Perfect, deaf, colorless
life is confirmed for me—
I feel it, certain, lightless:
the deep reality, matter.

Partial Eclipse, 1983. 8¼ × 12 in., charcoal on paper.

19

Valle

En el paisaje tierno
—aquí, quedarse—,
el puente de hierro.

Cielo azul, verde tierra;
el puente, ¡qué negro!

Sobre colinas muelles
voluntad en desmayo,
amor en vacaciones,
toda la vida en curvas.

Pero él marchar, seguir,
él, solo, puente, recto.

19

Valley

In this countryside that
holds on to you—stay here!—
the iron bridge.

Blue sky, green earth,
and the bridge, so black!

Will faints away
on the soft hills where
love goes on vacation
and life is summed up in curves.

Only the bridge marching on,
solitary, erect.

20

La difícil

En los extremos estás
de ti, por ellos te busco.
Amarte: ¡qué ir y venir
a ti misma de ti misma!
Para dar contigo, cerca,
¡qué lejos habrá que ir!
Amor: distancias, vaivén
sin parar.
En medio del camino, nada.
No, tu voz no, tu silencio.
Redondo, terso, sin quiebra,
como aire, las preguntas
apenas le rizan,
como piedras, las preguntas
en el fondo se las guarda.
Superficie del silencio
y yo mirándome en ella.
Nada, tu silencio, sí.

O todo tu grito, sí.
Afilado en el callar,
acero, rayo, saeta,
rasgador, desgarrador,
¡qué exactitud repentina
rompiendo al mundo la entraña,
y el fondo del mundo arriba,
donde él llega, fugacísimo!
Todo, sí, tu grito, sí.

Pero tu voz no la quiero.

20

Difficult Woman

You have fled to the extremes
of your self, where I look for you.
Loving you: so much going and coming
to you from you.
I'll have to go so far
to find you!
Love: distances, endless
swaying.
Halfway down the road, nothing.
Not your voice, no, your silence.
Globed, smooth, seamless
as the air; questions barely
graze that silence
like stones: it gathers
them inside itself.
The surface of silence
where I see my reflection.
Nothing, your silence, yes.

Or your whole scream, yes.
Sharpened by quietness,
steel, lightning, arrow,
suddenly ripping, neatly
splitting open the insides of the world,
striking for a second
the bottom of the world, turning it upward.
All, yes, all of your scream, yes.

But I do not want your voice.

21

Placer, a las once

El arcángel del domingo,
de paz arcángel guerrero,
estandartes desplegados
las horas de la mañana,
contra enemigo, el misterio.
Del hombro cuelga la aljaba
toda llena de alfabetos:
las letras que clavará
—¡qué propaganda del gozo!—
luminosas en el cielo.
Ya se le alistan detrás
voluntarios de lo cierto:
maquinaria americana,
ágiles volatineros.
¡Cómo empuja el mar sus olas
de sonrisas contra ceños!
El niño blande su espada:
"¡Sí, porque sí, porque sí",
toda afilada de quieros.
Escuadrones de cien voltios
alancean los reflejos.
Y van las voces redondas,
lunas llenas por los cielos,
en su perfil encerradas
sin servidumbre a los ecos.
Caprichos salteadores
risueñamente le quiebran
la cerradura al secreto.
El secreto, cascabel.
Suena, solución perfecta,
suena la alegría dentro.

21

Pleasure, at Eleven O'clock

Sunday's archangel,
warrior archangel of peace,
banners unfurled
in the morning hours
against his enemy—mystery.
Slung over his shoulder
is a quiver full of alphabets:
he will shoot letters
—pleasure's propaganda!—
that light up the sky.
Now volunteers of certainty
line up behind him:
American machinery,
agile acrobats.
The sea pounds its smiling
waves against frowns.
The little boy brandishes his sword
sharpened with wishes:
"Yes, because . . . just because!"
Hundred volt squadrons
launch reflections,
and round voices move
like full moons through the heavens,
enclosed in their own silhouettes
but free of all echoes.
Whims like highwaymen smile
as they break the lock
on the secret.
The secret is a tiny bell.
It rings its perfect solution,
rings out the joy inside it.

22

Números

Tenías abecedario
innumerable de estrellas;
clara
ibas poniendo la letra,
noche de agosto.
Pero yo, sin entenderla,
misterio, no la quería.
Aquí en la mesa de al lado
dos hombres echaban cuentas.
Más bellas que los luceros
fúlgidas, cifras y cifras,
cruzaban por el silencio,
puras estrellas errantes,
señales de suerte buena
con largas caudas de ceros.
Y yo me quedé mirándolas:
—¡qué constelación perfecta
tres por tres nueve! —olvidado
de Ariadna, desnuda allí
en islas del horizonte.

22

Numbers

You had an innumerable
alphabet of stars,
August night;
you kept writing
brightness.
Not understanding your words,
mystery, I rejected them.
Here at the next table
two men were working on accounts
more beautiful than galaxies:
figures, flashing figures
crossed the silence,
pure wandering stars,
signs of good luck
with trains of zeros.
I stared at them
—what a perfect constellation:
three times three is nine! —forgetting
Ariadne, who lay naked
above islands on the horizon.

23

"Route Nationale"

¡Pronto, la luz, pronto, pronto!
Un negror agazapado
salta de los horizontes
y me confunde la vida.
Las seguridades dulces,
distancias, perfiles, formas
de un revuelo se las lleva.
¡Colores, colores míos,
amarillo, verde, rojo,
arrebatados cautivos,
en cárcel de nueve horas!
Aquel paisaje tan firme
¿cómo se rindió tan pronto?
¡Resístete, variedad
amada, tú, no te dejes,
no me dejes solo
en lo negro, raso, uno!

Con una vuelta a la llave,
en visiones de cien metros,
fragmentado, alegre, vivo,
los faros
me devolvieron el mundo.

23

"Route Nationale"

Quickly, the light, quickly, quickly!
Crouching blackness
leaps from the horizons
and shrouds my life.
In one blast it sweeps away
distances, profiles, forms,
all the comforting certainties.
Colors, my colors—
yellow, green, red—
taken captive
in a nine-hour jail.
That solid landscape,
how did it surrender so quickly?
You varied colors that I love—
keep fighting, don't leave yourself
or me alone,
in the blackness, in the open, one!

With a turn of the key,
in visions of a hundred meters—
fragmented, joyful, alive—
headlights
restored the world.

24

La distraída

No estás ya aquí. Lo que veo
de ti, cuerpo, es sombra, engaño.
El alma tuya se fue
donde tú te irás mañana.
Aún esta tarde me ofrece
falsos rehenes, sonrisas
vagas, ademanes lentos,
un amor ya distraído.
Pero tu intención de ir
te llevó donde querías,
lejos de aquí, donde estás
diciéndome:
"aquí estoy contigo, mira".
Y me señalas la ausencia.

24

Distracted Woman

You aren't here now. What I can see
of you—your body—is shadow, illusion.
Your soul has gone
where you will go tomorrow.
This afternoon it still offers me
phantom hostages, vague smiles,
languid gestures,
love already distracted. And yet,
your longing to leave has already
taken you where you want to be,
far from here, where you are
saying to me:
"Look! Here I am with you."
And you show me your absence.

25

Madrid. Calle de . . .

¡Qué vacación de espejo por la calle!
Tendido boca arriba, cara al cielo,
todo de azogue estremecido y quieto,
bien atado le llevan.
Roncas bocinas vanamente urgentes
apresurar querrían
su lenta marcha de garzón cautivo.

¡Pero qué libre aquella tarde, fuera,
prisionero, escapado! Nadie
vino a mirarse en él. El sí que mira
hoy, por vez primera es ojos.
Cimeras ramas, cielos, nubes, vuelos
de extraviadas nubes, lo que nunca
entró en su vida, ve.
Si descansan sus guardas a los lados
acero, prisa, ruido,
corren. El, inmóvil
en el asfalto, liso estanque
momentáneo, hondísimo,
abre. Y le surcan
—de alas, de plumas, peces—
crepusculares golondrinas secas.

25

Madrid—Any Street

What a vacation for that mirror in the street!
Stretched out facing the sky,
all shimmering and silent quicksilver,
carefully tied up and carried along.
Horns rasp with urgency,
vainly trying to hurry
its slow, captive-heron march.

But it was so free that afternoon, outside,
an escaped prisoner! No one stepped up
to look at himself. *It* is the one
who looks today; for the first time *it* is eyes.
What it sees are high branches,
skies, clouds, flights of stray clouds—
things that never came into its life before.
If the guards on all sides stop to rest,
the steel, haste, and noise
rush by. It lies still
on the asphalt, opening for a moment
a deep, deep pond
that dry twilight swallows—
fish with wings and feathers—
plow into waves.

26

Cinematógrafo

1. Luz

Al principio nada fue.
Ni el agua para en ella el pez.
Ni la rama del árbol para la fatigada
ala del pájaro.
Ni la fórmula impresa para casos de duelo.
Ni la sonrisa en la faz de la niña.
Al principio nada fue.
Sólo la tela blanca
en la tela blanca, nada...
Por todo el aire clamaba,
muda, enorme,
la ansiedad de la mirada.
La diestra de Dios se movió
y puso en marcha la palanca...
Saltó el mundo todo entero
con su brinco primeval.
La tela rectangular
le oprimió en normas severas,
le organizó bruscamente
con dos líneas verticales,
con dos líneas horizontales.
Y el caos tomó ante los ojos
todas las formas familiares:
la dulzura de la colina,
la cinta de los bulevares,
la mirada llena de inquina
del buen traidor de melodrama,
y la ondulación de la cola
del perro fiel a su amo.

26

Movie Theater

1. LIGHT

At first there was nothing.
Not enough water for a fish.
Not the branch of a tree for the worn-out
wing of a bird.
Not the printed protocol for a duel.
Not the smile on the little girl's face.
At first there was nothing.
Just the white cloth
and on the white cloth, nothing . . .
An anxious gaze
clamored mutely, heavily,
in the air.
The right hand of God stirred
and pulled the lever . . .
The whole world sprang forth
with its primeval hop.
The rectangular cloth
squeezed it into rigid shape,
organized it brusquely
with two vertical lines,
with two horizontal lines.
Before our eyes chaos
took all the familiar forms:
the gentle swell of the hill,
the ribbon of the boulevards,
the hateful look on the face
of the melodrama villain,
and the tail of the dog
wagging for his master.

El hombre tuerto sintió
que va a quebrársele el ojo
de cristal, a la embestida
de tantas y tantas visiones.
En el fondo gritó un erudito:
"¿Y la palabra y la palabra?"
Y todos los esfuerzos del mundo,
la fuerza lograda y gastada,
las máquinas maravillosas
para correr, para volar,
para amar, para aborrecer
se echaron a funcionar.
El primer día de la creación,
humillado, pobre, vencido,
se marchó a llorar a un rincón.
Pero ya el instinto acechaba
en los ojos de la mujer
—la cabellera suelta al viento—
y en el tejer y el destejer
de la tela del sentimiento.
Y el primer día de la creación
se levantó de su rincón
y vino a asomarse a la tela:
en la mano diestra llevaba
el primer corazón del hombre,
que era el último corazón.

2. Oscuridad

El arco voltaico deja
desparramarse su alma
y lo entenebrece todo
la luz, madre de tinieblas.
Ha vuelto la tela blanca.
Pero ya es otra; se hizo
tela maravillosa.

The one-eyed man felt
as though his glass eye
would break from the attack
of so many visions.
In the back a purist yelled out:
"And the words, what about the words?"
Then all the energies of the world,
powers achieved and lost,
the marvelous mechanisms
for running, for flying,
for loving, for hating,
began working.
The first day of creation—
humbled, impoverished, beaten,
retreated to a corner to cry.
But instinct was already spying
in the eyes of the woman
—hair flying in the wind—
and in the weaving and unraveling
of the fabric of feeling.
The first day of creation
rose from its corner
and came to look at the cloth:
in the right hand it was carrying
the first heart of man,
which was the last heart.

2. DARKNESS

The voltaic arc allows
its soul to spill over
and light, the mother of shadows,
darkens everything.
The white cloth has returned.
But now it is different; it has become
a magic cloth.

Entre hilo e hilo de su trama
está encerrada toda cosa
y guarda avara
el mundo entero perdido.
Ya todas las almas sienten
su curso como de estrellas
que vivieron en valles floridos de la tierra
y besaron labios humanos.
Ahora vueltas al espacio
extaterrenal
siguen rodando hasta el día
que el destino astral las torne
a acercar al mundo puro,
la tela blanca.

It has captured everything
between one thread and another of its weave,
where it hoards
the whole lost world.
Now all souls feel
their trajectories, as if they were stars
that had lived in flowering valleys on earth
and kissed human lips.
Back in extraterrestrial
space
they keep spinning until the day
in which starry destiny returns them
to that pure world
of the white cloth.

27

35 bujías

Sí. Cuando quiera yo
la soltaré. Está presa
aquí arriba, invisible.
Yo la veo en su claro
castillo de cristal, y la vigilan
—cien mil lanzas—los rayos
—cien mil rayos—del sol. Pero de noche,
cerradas las ventanas
para que no la vean
—guiñadoras espías—las estrellas,
la soltaré. (Apretar un botón.)
Caerá toda de arriba
a besarme, a envolverme
de bendición, de claro, de amor, pura.
En el cuarto ella y yo no más, amantes
eternos, ella mi iluminadora
musa dócil en contra
de secretos en masa de la noche
—afuera—
descifraremos formas leves, signos,
perseguidos en mares de blancura
por mí, por ella, artificial princesa,
amada eléctrica.

27

35 Candle Power

Yes. When I feel like it,
I'll let her go. She's trapped
up here, invisible.
I see her in her transparent
castle of glass where a hundred thousand spears—
the rays, a hundred thousand rays of sun—
watch over her. But at night
when the windows are closed
so the stars
—winking spies—cannot see her,
I'll let her loose. (Flip a switch.)
She will fall all over me
with her purity and her kisses, wrap me
in blessings, in brightness, in love.
Just she and I in the bedroom, lovers
forever; the docile muse
who lights up the mass of secrets
from the night outside
will decipher with me subtle shapes
and signs pursued in seas of whiteness
by me, by her, my artificial princess,
my electric love.

28

Soledades de la obra

"Voy a hacer." (¡Qué mío es
lo que voy a hacer!)
"Estoy haciendo." (¡Qué mío!)
"Ya está hecho. Míralo"
¡Cuidado!
El hacer, enajenar,
quedarse solo, de hacer.
Salta, vuela, ya no es tuyo.
Solo.
Solo sin lo mío hecho.
Solo de lo mío, de eso
que hice yo, que me inventé
para no estar solo.
Forma de mis soledades,
yo me la estaba labrando.
Escapada.

La hice con ansias, con alas
de ansias. Se va
detrás de otras ansias, suyas,
poblando los cielos, suyos.
Y entre todo lo que hice,
mío, ya ajeno, ya lejos,
qué solo estaría hoy
sin eso, enorme, infinito,
de nadie, que me acompaña:
lo que aún está por hacer,
lo que yo podría hacer.

¡Y mientras lo hiciera, mío!

28

Solitudes of Creation

"I am going to create." (All mine,
what I make!)
"I am creating." (All mine!)
"Now it's done. Look at it!"
Careful!
To create is to alienate,
to isolate oneself through activity.
The work leaps up, flies away, is no longer yours.
Alone.
Alone without the work that I have done,
alone without what is mine, what I have invented
so as not to be alone.
I was giving form
to my solitude,
escaping from it.

I made it out of desire, wings
of desire. It goes
after other desires, its own,
inhabiting the skies, its own skies.
And in the midst of everything I've done,
my work now strangely alien, far away,
how alone I would be today
if not for that enormous, infinite
thing belonging to no one, accompanying me:
what is still undone,
what I could create.

And what was mine in the act of creation!

29

Más

¿Qué voy a ponerte a ti:
galeras de fantasía,
azahar falso, sombra falsa?

¿Qué voy a ponerte a ti,
tarde del día catorce,
si tú ya lo tienes todo:
naranjo sin flor ni fruto,
mar sin vela, luz de agosto?
En tu perfección parada,
inmóvil, así, dejarte
salvada de tu pasar,
quisiera.

Eternidad te pondría.

29

More

What can I give you?
Galleons of fantasy,
fake orange blossoms, false shadows?

What could I add to you,
afternoon of the fourteenth,
when you already have everything:
orange trees without flower or fruit,
sea without sail, light of August?

I would like to leave you
as you are, motionless,
poised in your perfection,
saved from your evanescence.

I would give you eternity.

30

Inminencia

Yo silencioso. Pero
grito, quejido, o risa
dentro y en pie con la ballesta armada.

Yo en tierra. Pero el barco
listo y los huracanes que me lleven.

Yo quieto. Pero
aquí a los cuatro lados, cuatro tajos.
Yo nada, sombra, pasajero y aire.

Pero, ¡tantos rumbos seguros!
Pero, ¡tantos soles eternos!

Pero, ¡tantas calmas augustas!
Para mí, sombra, pasajero y aire,
hoy.

30

Imminence

I am silent. But
one scream, cry or laugh
inside and I'm on my feet with crossbow drawn.

I am on land. But the boat
is ready and let the hurricanes sweep me away.

I am quiet. But
here, on all four sides, four cliffs.
I am nothing, shadow, traveler, and wind.

But so many safe paths!
But so many everlasting suns!

But so many calm radiant days!
For me, shadow, traveler, and wind
today.

31

Clave de febrero

Ni rosa en el rosal
ni tibieza en el viento,
pero está aquí, lo sé,
primavera del frío,
toda jugo en lo seco.
Sigilosa, invisible,
doctora en disimulos,
la gloria de mañana
es ya esta tarde suya.
Como llega sin fuerzas
¿quién la resistiría?
Desarmada
triunfo y filo previene;
no quiere nada, pero
querré lo que ella quiera.
En febrero me rindo;
a su núbil imperio
—el pecho apunta apenas—,
resistencias ahorro.

31

The Key to February

Not a rose on the rosebush,
no warmth in the wind,
but she's here, I know it:
cold weather spring,
the juice inside the dryness.
Secretive, invisible,
doctor of disguise,
the loveliness of morning
is hers this afternoon.
She arrives with no troops,
so who could resist her?
Unarmed,
she saves us from sword and conquest;
she wants nothing, but
I will want whatever she wants.
In February I surrender;
facing her nubile empire
—her breast barely touches me—,
I hoard my resistance.

32

Acuarela

Con el cielo gris
la copla
triste de Sevilla
se afina, se afina.
En agua sin sol
sombras de naranjos
entierran azahares.
Arriba,
en las altas miras
esperan las niñas
los barcos de oro.
Abajo
aguardan los mozos
que se abran cancelas
a patios sin fondo.
Sin rubor se quedan,
pálidas, las torres.
Desde las orillas
las desesperadas
luces suicidas
al río se lanzan.
Cadáveres lentos
rosa, verde, azul,
azul, verde, rosa
se los lleva el agua.

32

Watercolor

The sad ballad of Seville
keeps tuning, tuning itself
to the gray sky.
Shadows from the orange trees
bury the blossoms
in sunless water.
Up above,
girls in towers
wait
for ships of gold.
Down below,
boys wait for gates
to swing open into endless patios.
The towers stay pale,
do not blush.
Desperate,
suicidal lights
throw themselves from the banks
into the river,
where their sluggish cadavers—
pink, green, blue,
blue, green, pink—
are washed away.

33

Amada exacta

Tú aquí delante. Mirándote
yo. ¡Qué bodas
tuyas, mías, con lo exacto!

Si te marchas, ¡qué trabajo
pensar en ti que estás hecha
para la presencia pura!

Todo yo a recomponerte
con sólo recuerdos vagos:
te equivocaré la voz,
el cabello ¿cómo era?,
te pondré los ojos falsos.

Tu recuerdo eres tú misma.
Ahora ya puedo olvidarte
porque estás aquí, a mi lado.

33

Lover Beside Me

You facing me, me looking
at you. What a wedding,
yours and mine, to exact reality.

If you leave, it will be hard
to imagine you: you are designed
for pure presence.

I'll have to reconstruct you
with just a few vague memories:
I won't get your voice right,
and your hair . . . what was it like?
I'll give you other eyes.

You are my memory of you.
Now I can forget you
because you're here at my side.

34

La concha

Tersa, pulida, rosada
¡cómo la acariciarían,
sí, mejilla de doncella!

Entreabierta, curva, cóncava,
su albergue, encaracolada,
mi mirada se hace dentro.
Azul, rosa, malva, verde,
tan sin luz, tan irisada,
tardes, cielos, nubes, soles,
crepúsculos me eterniza.

En el óvalo de esmalte
rectas sutiles, primores
de geometría en gracias,
la solución le dibujan,
sin error, a aquel problema
propuesto
en lo más hondo del mar.

Pero su hermosura, inútil,
nunca servirá. La cogen,
la miran, la tiran ya.
Desnuda, sola, bellísima
la venera, eco de mito,
de carne virgen, de diosa,
su perfección sin amante
en la arena perpetúa.

34

Conch

Smooth, polished, rosy—
people would love to caress her,
yes, like a young girl's cheek.

I squint inside—my vision
curving, concaving, spiraling—
until I find her hiding place:
blue, rose, mauve, green,
unlit and iridescent like
evenings, skies, clouds, suns,
sunsets. It makes me eternal.

Subtle lines, geometric
elegances slope gracefully
in the enamel oval,
sweep unerringly toward
solution of that riddle
posed
at the bottom of the sea.

But her beauty will never be
good for anything. People pick her up,
look at her, then throw her away.
Naked, solitary, exquisite
shell, echo of myth,
of virgin flesh, of goddess.
Without a lover, she reproduces
her perfection in the sand.

35

Sur, con viento

¡Ay, Sevilla, Sevilla,
guerrera mala, dime
por qué todas las tardes
tantas saetas, me las clavas,
rebrillo de azulejos,
desde tus espadañas!
¡Ay, Sevilla, Sevilla!
¿Por qué secas al sol
ventolero de marzo,
blancas
brindadoras de paces,
camisillas de niño
banderas de la tarde
en altas azoteas?
¡Ay, Sevilla, Sevilla,
quiéreme por amigo!
Y Sevilla me quiso.
Y vinieron sus mozas.
Y heridas de saetas
—rebrillos—,
me las vendaban ellas,
con vendas
de camisas de niños,
secas
en altas azoteas.

35

South, with Wind

Oh, Seville, Seville,
cruel warrior, tell me
why you pierce me each afternoon
with so many arrows,
shafts of light from
the blue tiles of your towers!
Oh, Seville, Seville!
Why do you dry those
white
harbingers of peace
in the windy March sun,
those little children's shirts,
afternoon flags
on the rooftops?
Oh, Seville, Seville,
take me as a lover!
And Seville loved me.
Girls came out
and bandaged
my wounds from the arrows
—shafts of light—
with bandages
of children's shirts,
dry
on the rooftops.

36

Mirar lo invisible

La tarde me está ofreciendo
en la palma de su mano,
hecha de enero y de niebla,
vagos mundos desmedidos
de esos que yo antes soñaba,
que hoy ya no quiero.
Y cerraría los ojos
para no verlo. Si no
los cierro
no es por lo que veo.
Por un mundo sospechado
concreto y virgen detrás,
por lo que no puedo ver
llevo los ojos abiertos.

36

Looking at the Invisible

The afternoon is offering me
in the palm of its hand,
made of January and fog,
vague distorted worlds
like those I used to dream
and now no longer want.
Today I would close my eyes,
not look. If I don't
close them,
it's not because of what I see.
It's because of a world suspected,
real and untouched, behind this world.
My eyes keep searching
for what they cannot see.

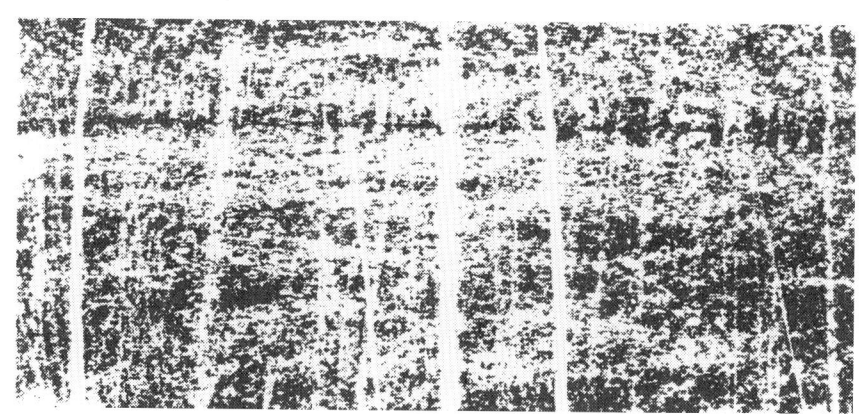

Ghost Trees, 1993. 4½ × 10 in., screen print.

37

Nivel preferido

¡Cómo se secaba el mundo
desde arriba, en panorama!
Mirador a mil cien metros,
doble asterisco en el Baedeker,
funicular y turismo.

Abierta de par en par
la vida por unas páginas
enormes, verdes, azules,
servicial, lisa, esquemática,
atlas
para mirarla tan sólo
entre los duros cristales
—vitrina— de las distancias.
Naufragantes van primores
espumas, yerbas, hormigas.
Sólo se salvan montañas,
mar, cielos altos, grandezas.
Ejemplos de lo sublime
sacaba una señorita
de una antología usada.

Y abajo, allí a media hora,
accidentes, dimensiones,
ruidosas delicias, números,
estaban ellas, mis gracias:

tu grito, grito, "¡María!"
¿Quién está llamando a quién,
con voz de por la mañana?

37

Favorite Altitude

The world in panorama
from above was getting so dry!
Scenic overlook at one thousand one hundred meters,
double asterisk in the Baedeker guide,
cable car and tourism.

Life opened wide
by enormous pages,
green, blue,
friendly, flat, schematic,
an atlas
that allows a glimpse of life only
through the hard glass
—showcase—of distances.
Subtle beauties, foam, grass,
ants are sinking out of sight.
Only mountains, sea,
lofty skies, grandeur are saved.
A young lady was expounding
examples of the sublime
from a worn anthology.

And down there, half an hour away,
were accidents, dimensions,
noisy pleasures, numbers,
all my joys:

your cry, cry of "María!"
Who is calling whom
in an early morning voice?

Letreros: "Salida", "Entrada",
sin puertas, sueltos, fatales,
como sinos, imperiosos.

Etiquetas de los precios,
sin más ni menos, exactas,
acabando con las dudas,
allí en los escaparates.

En la calle hirviente, clara,
a las doce en punto, sola,
una luz artificial
olvidada
en una ventana alta
—sólo yo la veo— flor
amarilla y torpe, errata
de las doce y de lo gris.

Y pregón, klaxon, bocina,
sin cesar, las hojas verdes
con que tejen las esquinas
invisibles
coronas para tus sienes,
ninfa de tacones altos,
desmelenada, tú, anécdota,
negándote por teléfono
a la cita que te di
en la bacanal, pintada,
del museo, de once a doce.

Signs: "Exit," "Entrance,"
without doors, free, fateful,
imperious, like destinies.

Price labels
there in the shop windows are
exact, no room for bargaining;
they do away with doubts.

Bright in the boiling street
at exactly twelve, just one
artificial light
left on
in a tall window
—I'm the only one who sees it—a flower,
limp and yellow, errata
of twelve o'clock and grayness.

And unceasing cries, klaxons,
horns, the green leaves
street corners use to weave
invisible
crowns for your head,
you, a nymph in high heels
with disheveled hair, a story,
turning down on the telephone
the invitation I made to you
in the museum's painted bacchanal
from eleven to twelve o'clock.

38

Lo olvidado

Estuvo aquí. Sí. Latidos,
corazón tierno de pájaro.
Yo le sentía. ¡Qué lucha
de caricia, roce, pluma!
¡Qué terca lucha suave,
ala impaciente en la mano!

¡Cómo gritaban los cielos
porque fuera y porque no!
(Había en medio una ronda
de acechadores neblíes.)

Ahora ya sin nada.
En la palma abierta el eco,
—tibieza—, de aquel calor,
de su contacto, brevísimo.

¿Llegaría allí, a lo alto?

38

Forgotten

It was here. Yes. The beating,
the tender heart of a bird—
I could feel it. What a struggle
against my caress—flailing feathers!
What a soft stubborn battle,
impatient wings in my hand.

How the heavens cried out
for it to fly away or not to.
(A patrol of falcons overhead
was waiting to attack.)

Then nothing.
In my open palm the echo,
—warmth—, from its heat,
from that momentary contact.

Did it get up there and away?

39

Sí reciente

No te quiero mucho, amor.
No te quiero mucho. Eres
tan cierto y mío, seguro,
de hoy, de aquí,
que tu evidencia es el filo
con que me hiere el abrazo.
Espero para quererte.
Se gastarán tus aceros
en días y noches blandos,
y a lo lejos turbio, vago,
en nieblas de fue o no fue,
en el mar de el más y el menos,
como te voy a querer,
amor,
ardiente cuerpo entregado,
cuando te vuelvas recuerdo,
sombra esquiva entre los brazos.

39

Recent Yes

Love, I don't love you very much,
no, not very much. You are
so certain, so mine, so safe,
so much a part of today, of this place,
that your obvious presence is the blade
that wounds me in your embrace.
I will wait to love you.
Your steel will soften and fade
in gentle days and nights,
far away, darkly, restlessly,
in clouds of *was* and *was not*,
in the sea of *more* and *less*.
How I am going to love you,
love,
love the ardent body you surrender
when you become a memory,
a fleeting shadow in my arms!

40

Aviso

Subir, bajar suaves,
por un paisaje verde.
¡Qué ruta fácil, toda
ondulaciones leves,
tarde larga, de prisa,
destinos en vereda
a los lados, sin fin!
Y de pronto la muerte
alta, recta, clarísima,
seria como una I.
¡Qué miedo frío dio
—dio, dará, da, daría!—
vista así, rostro a rostro,
ni esqueleto ni símbolo:
lineal, esencial,
muerte pura. En un fondo
negro, dos rayas blancas
que se cruzan, tres letras:
R(eal) A(utomóvil) C(lub).
Pero la vida pasa
—vencedor otro esquema—,
salvada en un triángulo:
freno a las cuatro ruedas.

40

Warning

Softly rising, falling
through a green landscape.
What an easy road, all
gentle undulations,
the long afternoon speeding by,
destinations branching out
endlessly on every side.
And suddenly death,
tall, erect, blinding,
serious as the letter "I."
It struck with such cold fear
—struck, will strike, strikes, would strike!—
that, seen face to face like this,
it is neither skeleton nor symbol:
linear, essential,
pure death. On a black background,
two crossed white stripes, three letters:
R(oyal) A(utomobile) C(lub).
But another destiny prevails
and life skids through,
saved by a triangle:
the brake against all four wheels.

41

Busca, encuentro

Llevo los ojos abiertos.
No te veo,
estás dentro de la niebla.

Niebla:
con el mirar no la aclaro,
con la mano no la empujo,
con el querer no la mato.
Niebla.
La mirada ¿para qué?
y la voluntad, inútil.

Llevo los ojos cerrados.
No te veo, ya te siento,
ya te tengo. Mía.
Estás, estoy, a tu lado:
estás dentro de la niebla.

41

Seeking, Finding

My eyes are open,
but I cannot see you,
you're inside the fog.

Fog:
I cannot see through it,
push it away with my hand,
kill it with my love.
Fog.
Why peer into it?
My will is useless against it.

My eyes are closed.
I cannot see you, but now I feel you,
now I have you. You are
mine, I am at your side:
you are inside the fog.

42

Marco

¡Qué cuadrado está el mar!
Tiene
costas inverosímiles,
cuatro lindes de oro.
Su corazón titánico
palpita en un espejo.
Tempestades copiadas
quiebran altas espumas
contra listones frágiles
que lo apaciguan todo.
Entras; y en el azogue
donde
tormenta septembrina
se ciñe, lucha y muere,
claro jirón se abre
al par —otro y lo mismo—
que te miras, sonrisa.

42

Frame

The ocean is so square!
It has
unlikely coasts:
four golden boundaries.
Its titanic heart
throbs inside a mirror.
Repeated storms
crash foam high
against fragile ridges
that calm everything.
You wade in, and in the quicksilver
where
a September storm
is surrounded, fights, and dies,
a bright shred of cloth unfurls itself
just as—different and the same—
you see yourself, smile.

43

El árbol menos

En el filo del hacha
me llevaron
un pedazo del mundo.
Ciprés:
largas sombras azules
en un muro encalado,
veo.
El ruiseñor cimero,
cantarín del antojo,
oigo.
Por su masa secreta,
índice vertical
del paisaje seguro,
sé.
En el filo del hacha
me lo llevaron todo.
Cierro los ojos
ante paredes blancas,
se me empapa el silencio
de ruiseñor huido,
tiemblo, inmóvil,
en campiña sin clave.

43

The Missing Tree

On the ax blade
they took away from me
a piece of the world.
Cypress:
I see
long blue shadows
on a whitewashed wall.
I hear
the nightingale at the top,
singing of desire.
By the tree's secret mass,
steady vertical index
of the landscape,
I know.
On the ax blade
they took it all away from me.
I close my eyes
before white walls;
the silence left by the fleeing
nightingale soaks into me;
I stand trembling
in a blank field.

44

Atalanta

Palabras que estás diciendo
—"cariño... siempre... seguro..."—
con voz lenta en gesto quieto.
Ventanas dobles, vidrieras
cerradas, encortinadas,
guillotinan tentaciones.
(Horizontes, aires, rumbos.)
El cielo es el techo, todo
del color que tú quisiste,
sin constelación ni guía.
Entreabierta alcoba —tuya,
mía—, renuncias desposa.

Pero más allá de todo
¡qué claro se te ve el sino!

Ni ese zapato de cuento,
de cristal, frágil, altísimo,
ni ese pelo ¡qué domado
plano, doméstico, liso!
me engañan. Ya se estremecen
las tierras que estrenarás,
el horizonte que rompas,
el cielo por donde subas.

44

Atalanta

Words you are saying
—"affection . . . always . . . certain . . ."—
with slow voice, quiet expression.
Shuttered, curtained-off
double windows
guillotine temptations.
(Horizons, winds, roads.)
The sky is the ceiling, all
in the color you wanted,
no constellations, nothing to guide us.
Door ajar to the bedroom—yours,
mine—that marries rejections.

But there, beyond everything,
your destiny appears so clearly.

Not even that storybook shoe,
the glass one, fragile, high-heeled,
not even that hair—so neatly
arranged, domesticated, smooth—
can fool me. The lands that
you will discover, the horizon
you may divide, the sky
you might climb
are already trembling.

Talón al aire te veo,
aquí tan quieta conmigo,
cabellera suelta al viento
—¡manzanas que te echaría!—
y luego
el mito ascensor antiguo,
que te sube, allá, a la fábula.

I see you, your heel in the air,
so quiet here with me,
your hair blowing free in the wind
—the apples I would throw to you—
and then I see
the myth, ancient elevator,
that lifts you into fable.

45

Pasillo de la prisa

¡Quémate día, quémate
en la —¡quémate día!— hoguera
de la prisa!
¡Pronto la llama alta
que me espera otro tú, otro día!
¡Más alta llama! Te echaré
porque te acabes antes
todo lo que me pidas.
Toda mi perfección guardada y seca,
ahorro de tantos años,
¡cómo la despilfarro,
viéndola chispear, brotar, chascando
para que ella me invente al consumirse
un mundo en blanco!
Desnudo del ayer, del hoy desnudo
¡qué ardiendo, qué saltando!
lo recordado —briznas—,
lo deseado —qué olor fresco de retama—,
en la hoguera lo veo. Yo lo eché.
Pero aún me quedo yo.
Derecho, yo también
a la llama, a la prisa,
a llegar, a pasar, limpio, por fuego,
más allá, al otro lado
—fénix, al otro día—
del día, de la prisa.

45

Path of Haste

Burn, day, burn
in the —burn away!— bonfire
of haste!
Let the flames soar,
for another you, another day is waiting for me!
Higher, higher! Day, I'll throw you in
so you'll end before
you make all your demands on me.
How I'm going to squander
all the safe and dry perfection
saved for so many years,
watch it shower sparks, leap up, crackling
and consuming itself
to invent a blank world!
That world—naked of yesterday and today,
burning and leaping
with memories (splinters),
with wishes (the fresh smell of shrubs)—
is what I see in the bonfire. I threw it in,
but I am still here.
Straight into the flames
I'll go, into haste,
and slip cleanly through fire
and get across—a phoenix—to the next day,
to the other side of this day,
the other side of haste.

46

Los despedidos

Tarde afilada y seca
corta como un cuchillo.
¡Unidad de mi alma!

En un siempre se hinca:
el tiempo, que era un siempre,
partido: ayer, mañana.
Y aquella sombra sola,
única, por la arena,
truncada en dos: tú y yo.

Secos rasgos, los vientos
firman sentencias últimas
de setiembre, destinos.
Aquí el tuyo, allí el mío.

Adioses, sin adiós,
ni pañuelo. El acero
del otoño la vida
nos parte en dos mitades.
La vida
toda entera, dorada,
redonda, allí colgando
en la rama de agosto
donde tú la cogiste.

46

Goodbyes

The dry afternoon tapers off
and cuts—oneness of my soul!—
like a knife.

It plunges into an always:
time, which was an always,
is divided into yesterday, tomorrow.
And that lonely shadow,
the only one on the sand,
is split in two: you and me.

The winds sign in dry strokes
the fatal verdicts
of September, destinies.
Here is yours, there is mine.

Goodbyes without goodbye
or even a handkerchief. The steel blade
of autumn slices
our life in two halves.
That life,
perfectly whole, golden,
round, hanging there
on the branch of August
where you picked it.

47

Fe mía

No me fío de la rosa
de papel,
tantas veces que la hice
yo con mis manos.
Ni me fío de la otra
rosa verdadera,
hija del sol y sazón,
la prometida del viento.
De ti que nunca te hice,
de ti que nunca te hicieron,
de ti me fío, redondo
seguro azar.

47

My Faith

I don't trust the rose
of paper
that I made so often
with my hands.
Nor do I trust the other
rose, the true one,
daughter of sun and season,
bride of the wind.
I trust in you, whom I never made,
in you, whom others never made,
in you, round
certain chance.

48

Amiga

Para cristal te quiero,
nítida y clara eres.
Para mirar al mundo,
a través de ti, puro,
de hollín o de belleza,
como lo invente el día.
Tu presencia aquí, sí,
delante de mí, siempre,
pero invisible siempre,
sin verte y verdadera.
Cristal. ¡Espejo, nunca!

48

Friend

I want you to be my crystal,
you're so bright and clear.
I want to look through you
to the world's essence
of soot or beauty,
whichever way the day invents it.
Your presence here, yes,
always facing me
but always invisible,
true presence without my seeing you.
Crystal. Never a mirror!

49

Playa

Flotante, sin asidero,
nadador fuera del agua,
voluntario a la deriva,
por las horas, por el aire,
por el haz de la mañana.
Todo fugitivo, todo
resbaladizo, se escapa
de entre los dedos el mundo,
la tierra, la arena. Nubes,
velas, gaviotas, espumas,
blancuras desvariadas,
tiran de mí, que las sigo,
que las dejo. ¿Estoy, estaba,
estaré? Pero sin ir,
sin venir, quieto flotando
en aquí, en allí, en azul.
Una alegría que es
el filo de la mañana
rompe, corta, desenreda
nudos, promesas, amarras.
Tropeles de sombras ninfas
huyendo van de sus cuerpos
en islas desenfrenadas.
Con su cargamento inútil
de recuerdos y de plazos
—¡ya no sirven, ya no sirven!—
el tiempo leva las anclas.

49

Beach

Floating, untied,
a swimmer out of water,
a drifter by choice
through the hours, through the air,
through the face of morning.
Everything is fugitive, elusive—
the world, the earth, the sand
slip through my fingers. Clouds,
sails, seagulls, foam,
crazy shades of white
attract me whether I follow
or ignore them. Am I, was I,
will I be? But without coming
or going—floating quietly
in here, in there, in the blue.
A joy that is
the edge of morning
rips, cuts, unravels
knots, promises, cables.
Throngs of nymph-like shadows
flee from their bodies
on wild islands.
With its useless cargo
of memories and schedules—
no good at all now—
time weighs anchor,

No se le ve ya. Sin tiempo,
prisa y despacio lo mismo,
¡qué de prisa, qué despacio
juegan los lejos a cercas
colgados del verdiazul
columpio de las distancias!
Su silencio echan a vuelo
enmudecidas campanas
y cumplen su juramento
los horizontes del alba:
la vida toda de día,
sin lastre, pura, flotando
ni en agua, ni en aire, en nada.

fades from view. Without time,
fast and slow are the same;
how quickly, how slowly
things far away seem near,
hanging on the bluegreen
swing of distances.
Hushed bells
send their silence into flight,
and dawn's horizons
keep their promise:
all of life this day,
free, without ballast, floating
not in water, not in air—in nothing.

50

Triunfo suyo

No se le ve,
pero está detrás, seguro,
imperial rostro insufrible,
dueño de lo último.
Aunque me deje ganar
fingidamente un instante
¡qué falsa siento mi fuerza,
que él me presta contra él!
Yo lo sé:
lo mío no es mío, es suyo.
Lo eterno, suyo. Vendrá
—¡que bien lo siento!— por ello.
Voy a verle cara a cara:
porque ya se está quitando,
porque está tirando ya,
los cielos, las alegrías,
los disimulos, los tiempos,
las palabras, antifaces
leves que yo le ponía
contra —¡irresistible luz!—
su rostro de sin remedio
eternidad, él, silencio.

50

His Triumph

You can't see him
but he's back there, safe,
with his imperial, insufferable face,
the lord of finality.
Though he may allow
the impression of a moment's victory,
the power he allows me against himself
feels completely bogus.
I know:
what is mine is not mine, it's his.
The eternal things are his. He'll come
for them—how well I know that!
I am going to see him face to face
because he is already taking off
and throwing away
heavens, joys,
illusions, times,
words, the thin masks
that I placed
against—irresistible light!—
his face of unavoidable
eternity, against him: silence.

Bibliography

Previous Translations:

Barnstone, Willis. *My Voice Because of You* (*La voz a ti debida*). Preface by Jorge Guillén. Albany: State University of New York Press, 1976.

Helman, Edith Fishtine. *Reality and the Poet in Spanish Poetry* (*La realidad y el poeta*). Introduction by Jorge Guillén, translated by Elias L. Rivers. Westport, Conn.: Greenwood Press, 1966.

Helman, Edith, and Norma Farber. *To Live in Pronouns*. New York: Norton, 1974.

Turnbull, Eleanor L. *Lost Angel, and Other Poems*. Preface by Pedro Salinas. Baltimore: The Johns Hopkins University Press, 1938.

———. *Sea of San Juan: A Contemplation* (*El contemplado*). Boston: Humphries, 1950.

———. *Truth of Two, and Other Poems* (Selections from *La voz a ti debida* and *Razón de amor*). Baltimore: The Johns Hopkins University Press, 1940.

———. *Zero*. Baltimore: Contemporary Poetry, 1947.

Valis, Noël Valis. *Prelude to Pleasure* (*Víspera del gozo*). Lewisburg, PA: Bucknell University Press, 1993.

A Selection of Critical Studies:

Allen, Rupert C. *Symbolic Experience: A Study of Poems by Pedro Salinas*. University: University of Alabama Press, 1982.

Barbagallo, Antonio. "Elementos futuristas en la poesía de Pedro Salinas." *Journal of Interdisciplinary Literary Studies* 3:2 (1991): 151–59.

Benson, Douglas K. "El amor contra la nada: Pedro Salinas, Francisco Brines y la tradición clásica española." *Revista Canadiense de Estudios Hispánicos* 15:1 (1990): 1–18.

Bou, Enric, and Elena Gascon-Vera, eds. *Signo y memoria: Ensayos sobre Pedro Salinas*. Madrid: Pliegos, 1993.

Breitenbucher, Alba. "El vocabulario del neoplatonismo en la obra poética de Pedro Salinas." *Revista de Estudios Hispánicos* 17–18 (1990–1991): 93–98.

Bruflat, Alan S. "Entre la fábula y el signo de Pedro Salinas." *Explicación de Textos Literarios* 19:2 (1990–91): 8–15.

Carreño, Antonio. "Los mitos del yo lírico: *La voz a ti debida* de Pedro Salinas." *La Torre* 7:26 (1993): 189–212.

Casalduero, Joaquín. "La creación poético de Pedro Salinas." *Cuadernos Hispanoamericanos* 431 (May 1986): 103–17.

Ciplijauskaite, Birute. "Pedro Salinas, siervo de amor: Poesía y vida." *Revista de Occidente* 126 (November 1991): 91–105.

Cowes, Hugo W. "El problema del referente en el discurso lírico de Pedro Salinas." *Actas del X Congreso de la Asociación de Hispanistas, I–IV*, vol. 2, pp. 1699–1706. Barcelona: Promociones y Publicaciones Universitarias, 1992.

Crispin, John. "Hacia una nueva edición de Pedro Salinas." In *Pedro Salinas: Estudios sobre su praxis y teoría de la escritura*, edited by Ciriaco Morón Arroyo and Manuel Revuelta Sanudo, 59–73. Santander: Sociedad Menéndez Pelayo, 1992.

———. "Metáfora y mito en la Generación de 1927: El caso de Pedro Salinas." *Journal of Spanish Studies: Twentieth Century* 6 (1978): 107–22.

———. *Pedro Salinas*. New York: Twayne, 1974.

Crispin, Ruth. "The Poetry of Absence: Salinas's *Razón de amor*." *RLA* 3 (1991): 402–5.

Debicki, Andrew P. "Construction and Deconstruction: The Theme of Fleetingness in Poems by Juan Ramón Jiménez and Pedro Salinas." *Studies in Twentieth Century Literature* 7:2 (1983): 115–24.

———. *Pedro Salinas*. Madrid: Taurus, 1976.

———. "The Play of Difference in the Early Poetry of Pedro Salinas." *MLN* 100:2 (1985): 265–80.

Delgado, Fernando G. "Apuntes para una nueva lectura de la poesía de Pedro Salinas." *Revista de Occidente* 126 (1991): 165–73.

Escartín Gual, Montserrat. "El uso de los tópicos literarios en la obra de Pedro Salinas." In *Signo y memoria: Ensayos sobre Pedro Salinas*, edited by Enric Bou and Elena Gascon-Vera. Madrid: Pliegos, 1993, 135–57.

Feal Deibe, Carlos. "Confianza y azar en la obra de Pedro Salinas," *Insula* 46:540 (December, 1991): 4–7.

———. "Lo visible y lo invisible en los primeros libros poéticos de Salinas." *Bulletin Hispanique* 93:1 (1991): 183–206.

———. " 'Thou Wonder, and thou Beauty, and thou Terror': La poesía amorosa de Pedro Salinas," *MLN* 94 (1979): 283–300.

Friedman, Edward H. "Poetic Duality in Pedro Salinas' *Seguro azar*," *Language Quarterly* 16:1–2 (1977): 51–52, 60.

Galimberti, Ana. "El ámbito de la luz en la poesía de Pedro Salinas," *Revista Chilena de Literatura* 43 (1993): 115–29.

Guillén, Claudio. "Pedro Salinas y las palabras," *La Torre* 3:10 (April–June 1989): 337–56.

Hatfield-Méndez, Vialla. *Woman and the Infinite: Epiphanic Moments in Pedro Salinas's Art*. Lewisburg, PA: Bucknell University Press, 1996.

Havard, Robert G. "The Reality of Words in the Poetry of Pedro Salinas," *Bulletin of Hispanic Studies* 51 (1974): 28–47.

Hierro, José. "Leyendo a Pedro Salinas." In *Pedro Salinas: Estudios sobre su praxis y teoría de la escritura*, edited by Ciriaco Morón Arroyo and Manuel Revuelta Sanudo. Santander: Sociedad Menéndez Pelayo, 1992, 41–58.

Marichal, Juan. "Pedro Salinas: La voz a la confidencia debida," *Revista de Occidente* 9 (1965): 154–70.

———. *Tres voces de Pedro Salinas*. Madrid: Josefina Betancor, 1976.

Maurer, Christopher. "Pedro Salinas y el lenguaje: Nombrar a la amada," *La Torre* 8:32 (October–December 1994): 601–13.

———. "Salinas y 'las cosas': Tradición y vanguardia," *Revista de Occidente* 126 (1991): 137–50.

Mayhew, Jonathan. " 'Cuartilla': Pedro Salinas and the Semiotics of Poetry," *Anales de la Literatura Española Contemporánea* 16:1–2 (1991): 119–27.

Newman, Jean Cross. *Pedro Salinas and His Circumstance*. San Juan, Puerto Rico: Inter American University Press, 1983.

Ortega y Gasset, José. "Miseria y esplendor de la traducción." *Obras completas*. Vol. 5, pp. 429–48. Madrid: Revista de Occidente, 1947.

Pozo, María del. "Mirar es buscar lo invisible: La poesía de Pedro Salinas," *Versants* 12 (1987): 7–28.

Price, Sandra. " 'Verdad de mitos': Some Aspects of the Use of Classical Mythology in the Poetry of Pedro Salinas," *Forum for Modern Language Studies* 20:4 (1984): 342–59.

Rubio Martín, María. "La forma métrica en la poesía de Pedro Salinas: Entre la microcomposición y la macrocomposición lírica," *Castilla* 16 (1991): 151–67.

Salinas de Marichal, Solita. "El primer Salinas," *Boletín de la Fundación Federico García Lorca* 2:3 (1988): 22–28.

Shaughnessy, Lorna. *The Developing Poetic Philosophy of Pedro Salinas: A Study in Twentieth Century Spanish Poetry*. Lewiston, NY: Mellen University Press, 1995.

Siles, Jaime. "La poesía primera de Salinas y la postmodernidad: Notas para un catálogo de semicoincidencias," *Revista de Occidente* 126 (1991): 151–57.

Silver, Philip. "Pedro Salinas y lo sublime romántico." In *Signo y memoria: Ensayos sobre Pedro Salinas*, edited by Enric Bou and Elena Gascón-Vera, 97–105. Madrid: Pliegos, 1993, 97–105.

Stixrude, David L. *The Early Poetry of Pedro Salinas*. Princeton, NJ: Princeton University, Dept. of Romance Languages, 1975.

Trueblood, Alan S. "The Poetry of Pedro Salinas in English." In *Signo y memoria: Ensayos sobre Pedro Salinas*, edited by Enric Bou and Elena Gascon-Vera. Madrid: Pliegos, 1993, 189–200.

Vila Selma, José. *Pedro Salinas*. Madrid: EPESA, 1972.

Young, Howard. "Jorge Guillén y Pedro Salinas: La verdad de dos," *Insula*. 48:554–55 (February–March 1993): 37–38.

———. "Pedro Salinas y T. S. Eliot: Dos posturas ante la modernidad." In *Pedro Salinas: Estudios sobre su praxis y teoría de la escritura*, edited by Ciriaco Morón Arroyo and Manuel Revuelta Sanudo, 75–95. Santander: Sociedad Menéndez Pelayo, 1992, 75–95.

Books of Poems by Pedro Salinas

Presagios (1924) — Foreshadowings
Seguro azar (1924–1928) — Certain Chance
Fábula y signo (1931) — Fable and Sign
La voz a ti debida (1933) — My Voice Because of You
Razón de amor (1936) — Love's Reasoning
Largo lamento (1936–1939) — Long Lament
El contemplado (1946) — Sea of San Juan: A Contemplation
Todo más claro (1949) — All Things Made Clearer
Confianza (1955) — Confidence